DYING WITH CONFIDENCE

DYING WITH CONFIDENCE

A TIBETAN BUDDHIST GUIDE TO PREPARING FOR DEATH

Anyen Rinpoche

Translated by Allison Choying Zangmo
Edited by Eileen Cahoon, PhD
Afterword by Tulku Thundup

Wisdom

Wisdom Publications
199 Elm Street
Somerville MA 02144 USA
wisdompubs.org

Library of Congress Cataloging-in-Publication Data
Anyen Rinpoche.
 Dying with confidence : a Tibetan Buddhist guide to preparing for death / Anyen Rinpoche ; translated by Allison Graboski ; edited by Eileen Cahoon.
  p. cm.
Includes bibliographical references and index.
ISBN 0-86171-656-6 (pbk. : alk. paper)
1. Death—Religious aspects—Buddhism. 2. Death—Handbooks, manuals, etc. I. Cahoon, Eileen Permut. II. Title.
BQ4487.A59 2010
294.3'423—dc22

                    2010025725

ISBN 978-0-86171-656-2   ebook ISBN 978-0-86171-924-2

21 20 19 18
5 4 3

Cover design by Phil Pascuzzo.
Interior design by Gopa&Ted2, Inc. Set in Arno Pro 12/15.8.

Wisdom Publications' books are printed on acid-free paper and meet the guidelines for permanence and durability of the Production Guidelines for Book Longevity of the Council on Library Resources.

♻ This book was produced with environmental mindfulness. For more information, please visit wisdompubs.org/wisdom-environment.

Printed in the United States of America.

Please visit fscus.org.

The essence of Buddhism is what is real;
what is real is what we practice
and what is in our hearts.
—Anyen Rinpoche

CONTENTS

—⚬⚬⚬—

Dedication   ix

Editor's Preface   xiii

1: Introduction   1

PART ONE: *Spiritual Preparations for the Time of Death:*
An Evolving Meditation on Life and Death

2: On Death and Mindfulness   11

3: Creating a Dharma Vision   19

4: The Dharma Will and Planning for Death   33

5: The Dharma Box   37

PART TWO: *Spiritual Practices as the Time of Death Nears*

6: The Bardos of Living and Dying   43

7: The Signs of Death   49

8: Liberation in the Bardos after Death   65

9: The Practice of Phowa   75

10: Instructions for the Practice of Phowa 83

11: When Death Is Near 93

12: How to Help Someone through the Dying Process 101

13: Liberation by Wearing 107

PART THREE: *Medical Considerations for the Buddhist Practitioner*

14: Buddhism and Western Science 113

PART FOUR: *Buddhist Practitioners as Caregivers*

15: The Entrusted Dharma Friend 123

Conclusion 131

Afterword by Tulku Thondup 135

Appendix I: Buddhist Prayers for the Time of Death 137

Appendix II: Documents to Prepare for Your Death 139

Appendix III: Sample End-of-Life Medical Instructions
and Dharma Will 141

Appendix IV: Resources for Legal Wills, Healthcare
Directives, and After-Death Care 155

Appendix V: Anyen Rinpoche's
Longchen Nyingthig Lineage 157

Appendix VI: The Meaning of Samaya 159

Index 161

About the Phowa Foundation 169

About the Author 171

DEDICATION TO TSARA DHARMAKIRTI RINPOCHE

You, who are indivisible from the primordial protector,
Father, accomplished mighty Dzogchenpa:
outside, you are the son of Shakyamuni
adorned by the three trainings;
inside, your heart is filled with bodhichitta;
secretly, you are the great, secret Vimalamitra.
Bestow the common and supreme accomplishments upon me,
a wanderer of the world,
so that I may establish the perfectly pure Dharma without hindrance.

Beings living in the modern, degenerate age
are continually tormented by five lethal poisons and drunk
on the five sense objects
following after fleeting worldly phenomena;

distracted by unattainable worldly actions;
believing that the insubstantial is substantial.
Protector, by your blessing and the mighty truth of the
Rare and Supreme Three Roots,
may all beings awaken from ignorance!
While in the Bardo of Birth and Living,
may beings first listen impartially to teachings,
then cut through doubts about the meaning,
and finally, take up the meaning that was understood.
May they follow after the sacred ones who have come before,
attain a fearless and confident death, and attain liberation
free of the bardos!
Especially, may they follow an authentic lama
with respectful body, speech and mind,
contemplate the view free of extremes and manifest
the uncontrived Mahamudra!
Based on realizing the meaning of effortless Dzogchen,
may they attain the stronghold of the Lineage of the
Longchen Nyingthig,
instantly accomplishing the stages and paths,
and reach the stage called Exhaustion of Phenomena!
Watch over me, blessed lama!
Watch over me, compassionate lama!
May the torment of the five poisons be pacified!
May all beings receive the heart of the sacred Dharma!
May they take up the path and put it into practice!
May they attain a fearless and confident death!
May the terror of the bardos be pacified!
May all attain Buddhahood, the primordial ground of the expanse!
AH! AH! AH!

KYABJE TSARA DHARMAKIRTI RINPOCHE passed away at the age of 90, on the first day of Sakadawa, 2005. Rinpoche had prophesied the month of his death six months prior, and passed away after giving teachings on the nature of birth and death. Just before he spoke his final words, he called the doctors and nurses around him and said, "Please remove the IV from my arm, and stop administering me any medication." He seemed to be telling us, *"This is how a true master dies."* Then, he spoke these final words, "At the moment of death, the ability to abide in the nature of mind, the indivisible three kayas— with its empty essence, clear nature and all-pervasive compassion— is extremely important." He spoke the seed syllable AH while seated in the vajra posture and then passed away.

Many miraculous signs manifested after Rinpoche's death. After Rinpoche's body was cremated, his bones became many-colored, glowing balls of precious medicine. The image of Tara arose from his skullcap, which did not burn in the fire. Rinpoche's body expressed the sign called *"tuk jak chen sum"* in Tibetan, or "heart, tongue, and eyes." This sign is attained by only the most superior of yogis, and was also attained by the omniscient Longchen Rabjam.

May all beings find inspiration in this story of Rinpoche's passing, and doing so, put the teachings into practice in their entirety.

Editor's Preface

My heartfelt request for Anyen Rinpoche to prepare this guide for dying came as a result of my own mother's death. As she lay dying over a period of seven months, I was drawn to Buddhist texts for advice on how to help her die skillfully.

The wish for her to be free of all her pain and suffering stirred deep in my heart. She'd had a stroke, and subsequently had shed those personality traits that had driven me crazy as a child; she was now transformed into a woman who radiated love at everyone she saw no matter who they were. I wondered if I could die too with such unconditional love.

My mother's death gave me the most precious gift of bringing me to Buddhism as well as helping me to recognize the immense opportunity we all have to share love and compassion, both in this life and at the time of death. It inspired me to learn more about the process of dying and how I could best help others go through it as well.

In this book, Anyen Rinpoche gives us practical information that will benefit both those seeking a Tibetan Buddhist death and non-Buddhists wanting to help a loved one or friend die in this tradition. He encourages us to take responsibility for ourselves as Dharma practitioners, to assess our practice honestly, and to contemplate impermanence—our own impermanence—deeply. He shows us how to create the necessary vehicles for using the process of dying to further our aspirations for enlightenment in the service of all beings.

Rinpoche has a grassroots vision of *"phowa* groups" throughout the Buddhist community practicing phowa, or the transference of consciousness at the time of death, both for themselves and for others. If a lama cannot be present at someone's death, experienced practitioners trained in phowa can be there to assist the dying person. Thus, through practicing phowa together, we can benefit our sanghas and Dharma communities.

There is, of course, much more to study in depth on this topic than can be presented in this one book—and ultimately, close contact with a teacher or lama is crucial. Nonetheless, by using the foundations in this guidebook, we can create the conditions for an excellent death and rebirth and make the most of our prior efforts to practice the Dharma and embody its principles.

I would have been grateful for such a guide to help my mother, and I am grateful now for these preparations for my own death and to help others. I hope we can all heed the advice given here, as we don't know when death will come.

The teachings in this manual were given in many different settings by Anyen Rinpoche since he came to America in 2005. They have been translated from the Tibetan by Allison Graboski, who is also the translator of Anyen Rinpoche's books *The Union of Dzogchen and Bodhichitta* and *Momentary Buddhahood.* Allison gave generously of her time and skills to not only translate additional teachings for this book, but to clarify numerous questions and offer wise insights. Without her untiring efforts in translating for Anyen Rinpoche, Western students would miss the opportunity to receive many precious teachings.

Rinpoche answers a number of direct questions from his students in this book that are relevant to Western culture and not addressed in traditional texts. I am very grateful that Rinpoche has agreed to continue to answer questions about the dying process on the website for the Phowa Foundation, a project of Orgyen Khamdroling, a non-profit organization founded by Anyen Rinpoche. The Phowa Foundation offers prayers and ritual practices for those who are ill, dying, or have already died, as well as retreats, education on the dying process, and special related materials.

Whenever Anyen Rinpoche gives teachings on preparing for death, the question-and-answer sessions could go on for hours. We are fascinated, curious, and a little uncomfortable all at once at the descriptions of the dying process and the bardo states. Part of this book grew out of just such question-and-answer sessions, and the gist of that material has been integrated into the flow of the chapters.

As we face the deaths of parents, loved ones, and our own unknown time of death, we will have many more questions that could not be included here. Students who may not have regular access to a lama will be able to benefit by asking their questions of an authentic teacher of Dharma, and exploring the resources and opportunities offered by the Phowa Foundation.

May this effort benefit all beings and help bring us swiftly to enlightenment.

Eileen Cahoon, PhD

1

INTRODUCTION

—⚭—

STARTING WHEN I was about two or three years old, I began to have experiences of death. One day, a woman named Kaki Padmatso came to my village. She gave me a walnut with a red-painted husk as a gift. It may sound incredible to a Western audience, but after I received that gift from her, strange things began to happen to me. I would stop breathing—and, one might say, literally die—for several minutes up to a half an hour. These death experiences continued to occur for about three years.

These were unique experiences in my life. Lama Chupur, the realized Dzogchen yogi who raised me, could not explain why this was happening to me. But he worked very hard to bring me back to the living, and practiced hard to release my life from the grasp of this obstacle. Although this could have been a very frightening time, the instructions I received helped me work through any fear I might have otherwise experienced.

One day, a poor, one-handed beggar named Pasang Lhakto came to our village. My mother told me later that Lama Chupur gave him all of the food we had in our humble kitchen—butter and steamed corn. Usually, my mother is a very generous person but on that day, Lama Chupur's generosity was even greater than hers. "What are you doing?" she asked him. Lama Chupur just smiled and said, "Your son will not experience this obstacle any longer." And I didn't. I did not experience death again until many years later.

Later, I felt as though the teachings on death and dying were, in a way, narrating the experiences of my childhood. I realized I had received an incredible gift: I know that what the Vajrayana Buddhist texts describe about death is what a being actually experiences before the inner breath ceases. I know that the descriptions given in the teachings on the bardos, literally *the intermediate states*, are accurate—and I know all this as a matter of personal experience. As a result, my trust in these teachings can never be shaken.

In 1997, I had another experience of death. I became very sick with pleurisy and fluid began to fill up my lungs. My body became very heavy. The Chinese doctor, untrained in any of the techniques of Western medicine, had never used a needle to remove fluid from the lungs before, but he decided he needed to do so now—and so he put a large needle in my back. No one knows exactly what he hit when he put the needle in, but I was unconscious for more than an hour. I didn't breathe for more than forty minutes.

I can assure you that when you are unconscious and not breathing, it is very difficult to recognize that you are dying and that you need to continue your Dharma practice. As I began to experience the stages after death, I was enveloped in heavy blackness. I don't know at what point, but suddenly I remembered my lama deeply in my heart, and began to pray to him. I was filled with devotion, and I thought to myself, "If I die now, I die with no fear. But if I am able to live, I will rejoice in that opportunity." Remembering that I had more work I wanted to do for the Dharma and for all beings, I thought to myself, "I am going to live and I am going to go back." With that thought, I was able to wake up again.

I can tell you it is very, very difficult to remember to practice at such a time. I can also tell you that it is sometimes even possible to "come back to life" if we recognize the state of death and then exert our will to live.

Throughout my life, I have remembered these experiences over and over again. I often reflect on death and the process of dying, and this has inspired me to begin working on projects to support those who are preparing for death. I feel that if practitioners have the same conviction about what will happen during the dying process that I do, they will feel more inspired to practice. Knowing what will happen when death arrives is so useful and practical—it is like a roadmap. After all, who wouldn't look for clear directions before they travel somewhere new?

We all know that death is certain—no one ultimately evades death. What we often forget is that death can come at any time. For Buddhists, the moment of death is the most potent opportunity to practice. Indeed, it is the key opportunity to attain realization or a positive rebirth. Thus, meditation practice in Buddhism is actually practicing for death. You are practicing so that you can have mindfulness and clarity in that moment when you are dying, so you are confident you are prepared to use the experiences after death for the best rebirth possible—or even complete and perfect liberation.

We must redefine the meaning of our practice so we can cultivate a feeling of *rejoicing* about the moment of death. If we practice hard enough in our lifetime, the experience of death will be our absolute best opportunity to have the strongest result from all of the aspirations and practices we've cultivated in our Dharma life. If we are duly prepared, I can promise that the moment of death *will* be an experience of rejoicing. If we are not prepared, it will surely be a time of fear and regret. When we think about death in this light, we should feel strongly motivated to practice every day.

Some people think that contemplating their own death will make them sorrowful. They would prefer not to think about it. For a meditation practitioner, however, this is a great mistake. By avoiding thinking about the reality and moment of death, we are losing a chance to really motivate ourselves to practice. We must reflect on our lives: there may only be a short time left. Do we have the confidence and the tools to die skillfully? Have we done the utmost to practice properly? Although we may plan how we would like to die and express our wishes to our friends and family, it may not always be possible to have someone next to us reminding us what to do. It is our responsibility to be prepared. No one can do this for us.

There is a metaphor in the Tibetan texts that says that one who receives teachings but does not gain experience through practice is like a farmer who doesn't tend his own fields—even as he constantly tells others how they should tend theirs.

People today receive many teachings, but at the time of death have they gained enough experience to die well? If we don't rethink how we are spending our lives and investing our energy in terms of our practice, we will be like the farmer and have nothing to eat at harvest time.

Preparing for Death

Students from many different cultural and spiritual backgrounds come and ask me for help when a loved one is dying. When someone close to us is dying or has died, we begin to think seriously about what our own death will be like. While this book will guide Buddhist practitioners preparing for their own death, it will also serve Buddhists and non-Buddhists who would like to help someone die while relying upon the supports of the Tibetan Buddhist tradition. Those who would like to help non-Buddhists in the dying process will also find these instructions useful and can adapt them to incorporate the spiritual tradition of the dying person—even if they are not Buddhist, they might appreciate your efforts anyway. And if they do not want you to perform *phowa* for them, you can instead generate compassion and pray for the person as much as you can.

For Tibetan Buddhists, however, unless you have extreme confidence or certainty about your ability to properly recognize and rest in the nature of mind, and unless you can rest in the Dharmakaya constantly, you should train in and practice phowa. It will not create any obstacles so it is always good to do. Furthermore, our assessment of where our practice is now may not be accurate. We may think that we are more skillful practitioners than we actually are. In light of this, it is best to practice phowa. What's more, it cannot be emphasized enough that everyone—practitioner and helper, Buddhist and non-Buddhist—will benefit by learning about the signs of death. Knowing what to expect will help us know what to do at the right time.

Before we learn the traditional Buddhist teachings on the signs and stages of death, before we take up the practice of the transference of consciousness, before discussing medical and spiritual considerations at the time of death—all topics we will explore together in this book—there are necessary preparations to enhance our chances of using these teachings effectively.

First, I am a strong advocate of each of us as Buddhist practitioners taking time for honest self-reflection and knowing where we are now on the spiritual path and where we would like to be in the future. Then I suggest creating two documents: one, a Dharma Vision, a realistic plan and commitment for accomplishing this lifetime's aspirations for practice; and two, a Dharma Will, a plan for how we wish to die that designates "entrusted Dharma friends" who have agreed to assist with rituals, prayers, and practices at the time of death. When people in the West get older, they write wills for their children. What we need now is a Dharma Will for ourselves!

After reading through this guide and creating your Dharma Vision and Dharma Will, I encourage you to prepare a special "Dharma Box" as well—this box should contain the Dharma Will, copies of our advance medical directives and other legal papers, as well as all the practices and ritual items we wish to have with us as we die.

I will offer specific instructions on using the different stages of the dying process as a spiritual practice and will also give detailed instructions on a phowa text that was passed down to me by my root lama, Kyabje Tsara Dharmakirti Rinpoche. This text is from the Longchen Nyingthig lineage. It is important to learn the visualizations now while you are healthy and sound of mind and body and able to practice energetically. This does not mean that phowa cannot be learned or trained in when we are elderly or sick, however, it is easier to master this practice when we are young and healthy. It is, of course, best to study with an authentic teacher and to attend phowa retreats whenever possible so there is appropriate support and sufficient time to experience the results of successful practice. The essence of all phowa teachings is the same, although there are slight differences in the texts. The phowa instructions given later in this book are sufficient to begin practicing now if you have not had prior instruction, or will serve as a reminder of any prior phowa teachings you have received.

Finally, we will explore the role of the entrusted Dharma friend and decide if we wish to serve sangha members and friends by practicing with them as they die and reminding them how to use the unique opportunity of death. I encourage each and every one of us to consider performing this service to our Dharma brothers and sisters. With very little effort, everyone can learn to do phowa successfully and contribute to the enlightenment of all sentient beings.

The phowa text and other practices to be recited as we are dying and to guide the consciousness after death can be found on the Phowa Foundation website at www.phowafoundation.org.

May these teachings inspire and guide us to practice the true Dharma and to face death fearlessly. May they help create the conditions for all to attain liberation and perfect enlightenment!

PART ONE

———— ⁓⁓ ————

Spiritual Preparations for the Time of Death:
An Evolving Meditation on Life and Death

2

On Death and Mindfulness

—⚉—

May the wisdom of our teachers' minds be transferred to our minds.
May we understand the teachings and put them into practice.

FROM THE MOMENT we are born, we are carried by four great rivers: birth, sickness, old age, and death. From the time that we enter the mother's womb until the actual moment of dying, there is no escape from this ordinary life into which we are born. No being escapes death. We all must die; we all *will* die—the only question is when.

The river of birth carries us to old age. No matter what we look like on the outside, we are all going to get old. We should not think that just because we are young, just because we are healthy now, that we have time. And we don't need to wait for the signs of death to appear; the signs of "far-away" death have already manifested for all of us! We have been born—that itself is a sign of death. We must therefore reflect on the fact of death now. If we do not think about it now, it will be difficult to think about it when it is happening—as it inevitably will. Most importantly, it will be impossible to have any kind of *mindfulness* that death is approaching if we refuse to reflect on it during our life. Through the cultivation of mindfulness now, the forces of habit and practice will help us practice it at the time of death. Truly, through the power of committed practice, there is nothing that cannot become easy. So if we put effort into reflecting upon death during our lifetime, we will find that this will support our practice and mindfulness at the actual time of death.

As the river of birth carries us to old age, it will also carry us along the river of illness, bringing us even closer to death. Reflect on all the various kinds of illnesses that exist on the planet today. Some are chronic and can make us ill for twenty or thirty years—or a whole lifetime. Some occur suddenly and are incurable. Some have gradual onset, so slow we barely notice until they are already very far advanced. As we get ill and closer to death, the "close" signs of death will begin to manifest. We can all recognize these signs if we train in mindfulness.

Many of you have taken birth in the country of America, where there is access to many material things. What is most needed, though, is access to true Dharma teachings. We may even have the good fortune to encounter the Dharma and to receive precious teachings, but often we lack the diligence to actually practice the teachings we receive.

Teachings on death and dying and on the transference of consciousness are supreme teachings. For ordinary practitioners, phowa is the teaching which is most accessible and which we are most capable of mastering. We should receive these teachings many times over, as often as possible. Doing so will strengthen our connection to that practice, which in turn will help us to be more present at the time of death.

The fact of death is certain. And for this very reason, because it is completely certain, death is something we should be fearless about. If we are not fearless at the moment of death, the only choice is to return to samsara, to re-enter the cycle of birth, suffering, and death, over and over again. We should reflect deeply on this.

In the Tibetan Buddhist tradition, many great lamas predict their own death far in advance. We wonder how they can do this with such certainty, often predicting the exact day they are going to die. One simple answer is that they have gained great experience in the signs of death and have such mindfulness that they can tell exactly when any of the senses begins to degrade. This allows lamas or yogis to abide in the profound teachings and do incredible things like dying in the posture of meditation, shrinking their bodies—a sign of nearly-complete realization—or even dissolving into rainbow body, a sign of complete realization. After their bodies are cremated, other signs appear, like the manifestation of *rangsel*, or luminous beads. The rangsel is able to manifest because these great yogis were able to abide in their lama's heart teachings at the moment of death.

In the West, old people are often placed in nursing homes to die. They don't want to depend on their children or accept help, and sometimes their children are just too busy to take care of them. If the children are in a position to offer care, their parents should accept it. Then the children can see every day how their parents get older and older; they can see the dying process. Then it becomes natural to think about death.

During our lifetimes, we generally pay a lot of attention to our bodies, but rarely think about what goes with us when we die. We cannot, of course, take any physical or material aspect of our lives with us when we die. It is only the consciousness that goes with us. It is also only the consciousness that experiences suffering or, more accurately, is able to perceive the experience of suffering. Most importantly, it is the consciousness itself that can be transformed into wisdom during the dying process. The majority of the time we are focused on maintaining our physical body and material environment, when we actually need to place our attention on practice! Realizing this can help us shift our focus and motivate us to practice every day.

An example we can use to understand this is the act of fainting. While the body and consciousness don't actually separate when we faint, we "lose consciousness" and as a result are not aware of what is happening with our bodies. Just like during the experience of the dying process, it is the consciousness that experiences everything, including our fears and our past experiences.

Thus, when we receive teachings on death and dying, or teachings on Dzogchen and Mahamudra, or any other profound Tantric teaching, we should never neglect or forget these teachings. They are essential instructions and we should try to reflect on them every day. If we are able to do that, we will remember them at the time of death and we will be liberated from the suffering of the bardos. If we do not reflect on the teachings, even having someone read the *Bardo Thodrol* (*The Tibetan Book of the Dead* or, literally, *Great Liberation upon Hearing*) to us at the time of death will not be meaningful. It will not stir that memory of something we did habitually during our lives.

Western students like to take a lot of notes at teachings, but I am not sure what happens to those notes after the student goes home. Condense your notes and make them truly your own; compose your own version of the teaching for personal use. Don't make something up, but write what your teacher taught you, in a way that is meaningful especially to you. Read it again and again over time. Then if a friend reads it for you as you are dying it will be easy for you to remember and actualize the essence of these teachings.

I have also found that Western Dharma students often want to do everything themselves. In this case, we should actually do so—we should take responsibility for ourselves by planning and practicing in such a way that we will be able to experience the death that we envision. We should also include others in our plan, allowing them to help us where it is appropriate. But, of course, if we do not practice with great diligence, having a plan for death is just pretending.

We may receive teachings and develop a close relationship with a lama, but we still have to practice. We must remember that when we do not practice, it is not for lack of time. Please don't deceive yourself in that way. We *do* have enough time. It doesn't matter how busy we are; we can find some time each day. Training to be mindful at the time of death is a step-by-step process. If we make great effort now, the signs of death will become signposts for practice and they will awaken our mindfulness when death is upon us.

I just learned to drive recently, so I need a lot of mindfulness when I am driving. But when I look around at other drivers, I see that they don't seem to need as much mindfulness. They have trained in this since they were sixteen years old; it has become natural for them. Dharma practice is just like that. Right now we need to practice mindfulness no matter what we are doing—walking, eating, sitting, sleeping, driving. Then one day we don't need to try to "have mindfulness," it will come naturally. It won't be hard to practice Dzogchen; it will be just like driving down to the grocery store!

Mindfulness training is actually based on the outer objects or conditions that are happening in the world around us all the time. When we gain experience, we begin to notice the kinds of outer conditions that make it possible to abide in meditation more easily. When we become skillful and recognize, "Oh, in this situation it is easy for me to meditate," or, "When I have these kinds of conditions or energy around me it helps me," this improves our mindfulness and our ability to abide in the view, to fully rest in the mind's primordial nature. It is very important that we make a study of the outer environment and our interaction with it as it relates to practice. This is something that acts as a general support for all kinds of meditation.

We need to work on summoning our motivation to practice and train hard in this life, as it will be very hard to remember our practice if we are sick or in pain. It is important to remember that practice and realization is not like a rock falling from the sky; it will not just suddenly hit us. We cannot attain skills in mindfulness and meditation instantly. Accordingly, we must not downplay to ourselves the importance of practice and training in mindfulness.

Mindfulness that is endowed with effort over time will naturally transform into effortless mindfulness. Effortless mindfulness endowed with *rigpa*, primordial non-dual cognizance, is a synonym for abiding in the view.

The Meaning of Confidence

Let me tell you a beautiful story about having a plan for death. When I was very young, I went to see a great Bon master whose lama had attained rainbow body. He was living in a tiny room and on the table was a small stupa. I was a mischievous child and I asked a lot of questions, so of course I asked him why he had that stupa. The master answered, "I have this stupa because when I die they are going to put my body in it." I looked at him. He was *huge*. So I asked, "How will you fit in that stupa?" The master said, "I will have to train myself to fit or there is no benefit to even having a stupa like this." This master had so much confidence, he was sure he was going to fit in the stupa when he died. This is real confidence in one's preparation for death.

I was told that the Bon master almost attained rainbow body. His body did shrink to a very small size, but one obstacle arose. He told his niece, who was helping to care for him, that when he died she must not open the door to his room for seven days no matter what happened. He made her promise that. She was very young, though, and after five or six days she thought, "I don't know what is happening to my uncle." So she opened the door and as a result, his body was unable to dissolve any further. If she had not opened the door, he would surely have attained rainbow body.

Maybe here in America we can put a security code on our door so that will not happen!

3

CREATING A DHARMA VISION

---—⟋⟍—---

Deepening Our Commitment to Dharma Practice

IT HAS BEEN more than fifty years since many lamas of my parents'
and grandparents' generation began to cross the borders of Tibet
and change the spiritual face of the West forever. The early students
of Tibetan Buddhism here in the United States, now my adopted
home, are advancing both in their practice and in their years. While
death can surely arrive at any moment, for many the truth of impermanence is just now beginning to dawn with some clarity, with some
certainty. The true test of their faith and practice is beginning.

While there is much debate and legitimate concern about how
Buddhism has adapted to the West—and vice-versa!—it seems
timely and useful now, regardless of our age, to focus on our personal
progress since taking up the Buddhist path. How have we changed?
How have we worked with obstacles that have arisen along the way?
Have we slipped back into any unwholesome habitual patterns and
not even noticed? What kind of faith do we find in our hearts right
now? What is our current commitment to practice? Where do we
want to be as Dharma practitioners at the time of our death?

These are not just rhetorical questions. Please ask them to yourself, right now. Take an honest look inside and recognize what you need to do to fulfill your spiritual aspirations in whatever time you have left. All of these questions together are what is meant by the question, "What is your Dharma Vision?" What kind of practitioner are you *truly* willing to become so that the moment of death fulfills the aspirations you have for enlightenment—or at the very least to take a rebirth that allows you to continue your practice and be in the presence of authentic teachers again?

Just as all of us make great effort to maintain our everyday lives, we should make similarly great effort in our preparations for death. If we are living and practicing the essence of the Dharma teachings, there should be no difference between our spiritual practices while we are living and those that we engage in at the time of death. One practice that we all share on the path, no matter what other teachings we have received or practices we have committed to, is training in mindfulness to ensure that in our last moments we will be able to make good use of our death.

We all seek to be the best human beings we can be. And regardless of our beliefs, death will come to all of us. Everyone can benefit from preparing for death as a spiritual practice. Additionally, if we learn how to support a loved one while they are dying, we will be giving them a great gift by helping them fulfill their own spiritual aspirations.

The Need for a Dharma Vision

Many of us on the Buddhist path have heard from our teachers that "the path is the goal" and that we should cut through any attachments to results. This is most true specifically on the path of meditation; we should not have hope for any particular experiences or signs of realization in our meditation. Hungering for such experiences will only bring us obstacles. Nevertheless, without earnest self-reflection and a vision for ourselves as practitioners, we will not really know how to take up the path.

In Tibet, few monks and nuns receive the teachings of Dzogchen, and even fewer laypeople are introduced to them. Here in the West, we expect the highest teachings to be given freely even if we have made little effort in the foundational practices. But it is the yogis who spend years training their minds, using self-reflection as a tool to further their progress, who become the highly realized practitioners.

We must be careful about having only the *appearance* of a Dharma practitioner. Some students who have received many teachings tell me they are "on and off" practitioners; they "sort of" practice and have little experience. Sometimes they are very passionate about one practice for a short period of time. They may burn like fire, but then something or other happens and they stop practicing. They lack certainty about what is the perfectly pure path. We need to abandon this habit of being an "on and off" practitioner. If we let our energy get too high, we can expect a counterbalancing low to follow when we lose our enthusiasm. Thus, in terms of Dharma practice, having a tempered passion is a more useful quality.

Because it is so easy to deceive ourselves about our practice, it is very important to have a relationship with a spiritual friend, a lama, who will help cut through any self-deception. But we must do our part to be prepared for and to nurture such a relationship; we must be diligent in our practice and have a realistic idea of our spiritual goals. Self-reflection can bring a new level of trust and mutual respect to an established relationship with a teacher by demonstrating that we are suitable spiritual "vessels," worthy of receiving profound lineage teachings. We can transform our outer trust in the Three Jewels—in the Buddha, in the teachings, and in the community of noble practitioners—into authentic confidence that develops unshakeable faith in the Buddhist path to enlightenment.

I consider the Dharma Vision, what we might call our spiritual aspirations, to be an evolving meditation on living and dying. It makes no difference what stage of life we are in. As practitioners, we need a guide for living as well as for dying that we can skillfully rely on during our lives as well as at the moment of death.

It's also important to include others in our Dharma Vision. Many of us, wishing to increase our expressions of loving-kindness and compassion, also want to help friends, loved ones, pets, and strangers alike die with the same opportunities for a "good death" that we wish for ourselves. If we do have the wish to help others through the dying process, we must first train ourselves to understand how our own lives move towards death. We must gain knowledge and wisdom about the process of dying that will enable us to use one of the most important moments of this incarnation wisely. Then we can make a serious commitment to becoming practitioners who take responsibility for accomplishing the vision of helping ourselves and others to die well.

At the end of this chapter is a special section with contemplations and guided meditations to help you develop and clarify your Dharma Vision.

The Dharma Will, Entrusted Dharma Friends, and the Dharma Box

When we understand the importance of the dying process and the potential we have for liberation during and after our death, it will be easy to see how essential it is to prepare properly for death. I would like to plant seeds here first for the ideas of a Dharma Will and of what I call entrusted Dharma friends.

I encourage students to form core groups of entrusted Dharma friends who agree to help each other through the dying process according to the wishes written down in each person's Dharma Will. The Dharma Will allows us to record our spiritual directives, so family and friends will know the kind of death we wish to experience and how it can be accomplished. Our entrusted Dharma friends should at least be familiar with phowa and other Buddhist practices. Once each person has written a Dharma Will, he or she can share it within the core group as part of training in recognizing the signs of death, mastering phowa, and learning how to skillfully help someone through the dying process.

Entire sanghas, or spiritual communities, can also pledge to help entrusted Dharma friends within their community fulfill their commitments. Each core group will need others from the spiritual community to assume some of the tasks involved in supporting the dying person's wishes, such as informing the sangha about appropriate prayers and rituals, practicing phowa together, and helping with funeral arrangements. This will be a wonderful way to strengthen our spiritual relationships and gain confidence in using the dying process for spiritual practice. Once we are skilled in phowa, a monthly or bimonthly group practice session can support the entire community's effort.

I also advocate creating a "Dharma Box," an actual box that will contain everything we and our entrusted Dharma friends will need to help us through the dying process. The Dharma Box will include copies of our Dharma Will and legal papers, ritual items, Dharma practice texts, and instructions for family and friends. Once the Dharma Box is complete, we can return to our Dharma Vision and engage fully in the practices we have committed to through the creation of that vision, with the assurance that we have put every-thing in place for the time of death. We'll explore the Dharma Will and the details of the Dharma Box in the next two chapters—what follows next are details for developing your Dharma Vision.

—⁓—

CREATING YOUR DHARMA VISION THROUGH CONTEMPLATION

There are many traditional meditations on death and impermanence in the foundational practices of all schools of Tibetan Buddhism. We can think about how the seasons change and how the elements of the world around us transform; we can look at how our bodies have changed from the time we were born until now; we can contemplate how our minds are constantly transforming. Reflecting on imperma-nence is the best way to prepare ourselves for the moment of death; please take some time to reflect on the contemplations below.

In the next few pages, I will suggest some specific questions for students to contemplate. It would be best to set aside a personal retreat day or weekend without interruptions for these practices, or to do this with your entrusted Dharma friends in a group retreat. You may want a journal to write down insights and ideas that arise as you do these practices. Some students have also found journaling helpful in tracking their progress in meditation and conduct over a period of a month or so and they use that as a basis for further reflection. You should decide what tools will help you the most in making this assessment of your Dharma practice.

Again, I encourage you to take an honest look at yourself as a Buddhist practitioner on the path. Sit quietly and cultivate a proper motivation. Generate *bodhichitta*—the wish to become enlightened in order to help others attain enlightenment—for all sentient beings. I suggest you read one of the contemplations below to yourself a few times over. Take time to consider it fully, keeping your mind focused but open to all ideas that arise. When you feel ready, rest in meditation free of reference points for as long as you can. When you finish your meditation, if you like, take time to write about your insights and experiences. Then continue with the next contemplation in the same way.

When you've thoroughly explored each of the contemplations below, you can begin to incorporate what you have learned about yourself as a practitioner into your Dharma Vision. Even if you have been practicing for a long time, you may be surprised at what you find lacking in your practice when you have taken an honest look. Many of my students find great inspiration in this process to increase their diligence and focus on areas needing attention. Don't forget to practice compassion for yourself. Appreciate the past efforts you have already made and include the efforts you are willing to make to become the excellent practitioner you have envisioned.

One of the biggest obstacles we might find we have as practitioners is that we lack a sense of urgency about the need to practice. This is caused by our strong experience of self-attachment. Self-attachment is expressed in many different ways. For example, we might think, "Let me just enjoy my life right now; let me enjoy this particular moment." We put off practice for a later time, which we fail to realize may never come. The best time to practice, the best time to prepare for the reality of death, and the best time to clarify our own Dharma Visions, is the present. Don't waste a moment.

Having a sense of urgency about practice could cause us to overestimate ourselves, however, or to want to skip over the hard work of developing a solid and stable base of daily practice. As you create your Dharma Vision, make an effort to balance idealism with realism.

We may all wish to be great yogis like Milarepa or Longchenpa, but our capacity is more likely to be one of an ordinary practitioner. We should reflect realistically on where we are now in our practice and what kind of practitioner we wish to become. We must be honest about our capacity so that our goal will not be beyond our reach. As I have stated above, we must also continually be mindful of life's impermanence and the reality of impending death. We may not have all the time we think we will have to practice.

We can aspire to such goals as receiving profound instructions from authentic teachers of all lineages and gaining experience and certainty in their meaning and in the primordially pure view of Dzogchen. We can always aspire to increase our bodhichitta and can do so by daily employing such practices as *tonglen*, in which we take in the suffering of others and send out positive wishes for healing and happiness in exchange. We all should wish to become proficient at practicing phowa for ourselves so that we may use it effectively at the time of our deaths, to die without regrets and with altruistic motivation for our next life. We may wish to become a practitioner who can sit with confidence with people who are dying and support them during the dying process. We may think about how we may help our teachers accomplish their Dharma activities and where we can contribute our talents.

Regardless of how we regard our talent for writing, we can all compose an aspiration prayer for the time of our death and include it at the end of the Dharma Vision. We can read this aspiration prayer before sleep each night so its meaning fully enters our hearts. Then, as we are dying, an entrusted Dharma friend can read this to us to remind us of what we are trying to accomplish and of our bodhichitta. A copy of this prayer can be kept in our Dharma Box, and buried or burned with us after we die.

IDEAS TO CONTEMPLATE

▶ *Contemplate Impermanence from the Outer Point of View*
Reflect on how your outer environment has changed during the past year. Recall how the seasons changed: how the plants, flowers, and trees transformed over time; how the daylight increased and decreased. Think about it both in your own personal living environment and throughout the globe as well. Think about the natural catastrophes that occurred around the world. Reflect on all the births and deaths of people, animals, and insects. Allow the enormity of these changes to reach you on a deep level until you feel with certainty that not even one thing remained the same.

▶ *Contemplate Impermanence from the Inner Point of View*
Imagine yourself as a small baby. See the physical changes you have gone through until now. Sometimes looking at photos of yourself from childhood to the present can be a poignant way to examine your own physical impermanence. Look at the transformation that has occurred in you physically. Then think about your physical being from last year until now, from last month until now, from yesterday until today. See that your body is changing even from moment to moment.

▶ *Contemplate Impermanence from the Secret Point of View*
Reflect on the wild nature of your own mind. Remember yourself as a child and how your intelligence developed over time. Look at how your mind changes moment by moment as it fills with entertaining distractions or follows after different sensory experiences. Contemplate how you are constantly transforming mentally and how the mind is also impermanent.

▶ *Contemplate Your Spiritual Practice*
Reflect on your daily practice. Are you practicing regularly and for as long as you would like? Are you able to incorporate all the practices you wish to master into your daily practice?

Reflect deeply on what type of practitioner you really want to be. What are the obstacles that stand in your way? Think about any tendencies you have that prevent you from practicing in this way. What is the main cause? Identify the things that cause you to put off practicing.

▶ *Contemplate the Impermanence of Things to Which You Are Attached*
If you are attached to material objects in the world around you, reflect on their changing nature. If you are attached to a person, reflect on him or her growing old and dying. Actually envision his or her physical and mental changes. If you are attached to your own life, as we all are, go through your body from the ends of the hair on your head to the tips of your toes and try to find anything that is lasting or permanent in your body. Do a very thorough examination, looking from outside to inside to see if you can find anything that is unchanging. Do this until you are confident that you, too, are actually going to die, and that you cannot hold onto this life forever.

▶ *Contemplate the Six Paramitas, or Transcendent Actions, Starting with this Past Month's Practice of Generosity*
Look at how you practiced during the past month and how you have integrated practice into your daily life by examining how you have expressed generosity. Were you able to give love, emotional support, or material goods without attachment? Was

your heart open unconditionally? If you compare this month to the previous month, was your generosity different or the same? If you compare last year to this year, have you been more generous? Less generous? The same? If you are the same, what will you do to increase your expression of generosity? If you have been less generous, reflect on why you have changed.

▶ *Contemplate this Past Month's Spiritual Practice in Terms of the Remaining Paramitas*
In the same way, examine your progress in virtue and morality; patience and tolerance; diligence and enthusiastic effort; meditative concentration; and wisdom. Take time to look at each quality and how you express it in your daily life. If you find yourself lacking in the expression of these enlightened qualities, make a plan to work on them. For example, make an effort to stay mindful of one quality over the next month and look for ways to enhance it. You will find many opportunities. Over time you can become habituated to remaining mindful and increasing the practice of each quality. You will find your daily practice improving greatly.

▶ *Contemplate this Past Month's Spiritual Practice in Terms of Anger*
It is very important to similarly contemplate your recent expressions of anger and resentment. These are the hardest to purify. Compare your expressions of anger and resentment in the past to how you feel currently. As a general trend, is it becoming easier to let go of them and generate compassion? If not, how will you work on this? Again, focus on anger or resentment by remaining mindful as these emotions arise. Work with any methods you have been given to cut through afflictive emotions. If this is difficult for you, ask your spiritual friend for advice.

▶ *Contemplate this Past Month's Spiritual Practice in Terms of the View*
If you have received instructions from your lama on abiding in the view, or the nature of mind, assess your progress during the past month. Were you able to remember to abide in the view one hundred times a day? Twenty-one times a day? Three times? Have you increased the number of times you remembered to practice? Has it become easier? If not, how will you improve your practice?

▶ *Contemplate the Importance of Mastering the Mind*
Your mind must deal with every experience. Think about how attaining mastery over the mind will enable you to lose any fear of death. Come to the certainty that you must master your mind in order to die with confidence.

▶ *Contemplate the Death of a Pet or Animal You Love*
Imagine that an animal you love very much is ill and close to dying. Or, considering what is happening in our world today, think that the last of an entire species you love is about to die. Recognize that animals have no way to take care of themselves spiritually or mentally in this situation. It is not that they do not want to; they are simply incapable of doing so. With compassion for their suffering, also reflect on your good fortune in being born as a human being who can take care of yourself emotionally and spiritually at the time of death.

▶ *Contemplate the Death of a Person You Love*
You may have already experienced the death of someone to whom you were very close. Perhaps they did not have all the spiritual support they needed to die without fear or regret. If

so, recall the experience of their death and again reflect on the good fortune that you are able to prepare well for your own death. If you have not had someone close to you die, imagine the death of someone you love and reflect deeply on your wish that they will experience no suffering and have all the support they need to die mindfully.

▶ *Contemplate the Causes and Conditions that Led to Your Birth and Will Lead to Your Death*
Recognize the long chain of positive and negative actions that brings you to this very moment. Search for a deep understanding of karma, causes and conditions, and how you can affect your spiritual path with mindful actions from now until death. Then consider the type of practitioner you wish to be at your death and what kind of spiritual support you will want from others. Take time to imagine yourself in the dying process. Do you have the confidence to die well? Are you ready?

Also, reflect on the idea that you may die suddenly, or during an accident. How can you be spiritually prepared for that experience?

▶ *Contemplate Difficulties with Your Death*
As you imagine yourself dying, do any obstacles arise in your mind that would prevent you from having the kind of death you wish? What are they and what can you do to remove them?

▶ *Contemplate Your Ideal Death*
What will your mind be like? What qualities will you have developed? What practice will be most important for you to do or hear at that time? Who do you want to be there to help you stay focused on your practice as you are dying?

▶ *Contemplate Your Level of Practice*
What changes do you need to make in your daily practice to best ensure you become the type of practitioner you want to be?

▶ *Contemplate Your Relationship with a Spiritual Friend*
If you have had the good fortune to meet and make a strong connection to a lama or spiritual teacher, reflect on this relationship and what it is like now. Have you developed the kind of relationship you envision? If not, what can you do to develop this relationship further?

REVISING YOUR DHARMA VISION

The Dharma Vision is a living and evolving meditation. We are always changing and growing in our understanding. I recommend that each year, perhaps at the new year or on your birthday, you commit to reviewing your vision as a Dharma practitioner, assessing your progress, and seeing if there is anything new you want to add. You may want to again return to the contemplations above. If you have done any of this work in a group retreat, it would be fruitful for everyone to meet again to review and share both your progress and your obstacles. Support each other with kindness and appreciate the efforts everyone has made. Your sangha and entrusted Dharma friends are most precious!

4

THE DHARMA WILL
AND PLANNING FOR DEATH

In Tibet, most people die at home surrounded by their families. And increasingly, this is starting to be the case in America as well, with a return to greater family involvement with the dying process and after-death care. I think this is very positive. Our Dharma Wills can reflect our aspiration for this involvement of family and entrusted Dharma friends and specify our wishes for the kind of death we have envisioned. With our legal documents and Dharma Wills completed carefully and our wishes clearly understood, we will be able to bring the mind's focus at death to our meditation practice.

All of us need to have a Last Will and Testament whose execution meets the statutory requirements of the state we live in. However, the Dharma Will we create for our spiritual care at death is not a will in the legal sense; it is, quite simply, a document stating our wishes for spiritual care as we are dying and immediately after our death. The Dharma Will designates the entrusted Dharma friends who will help us through the dying process, and is like a spiritual contract with Dharma friends for special conduct to be carried out. It also gives specific information for contacting a lama, expresses our wishes for burial or cremation, states what to do with our ashes if cremation is chosen, and makes plans for charitable contributions to private foundations and nonprofits that benefit our society, or to our lama or a monastery if prayers and phowa have been requested. Many Buddhist practitioners ask monasteries or lamas to perform phowa and purification rituals, make ritual offerings, and recite texts for a period of forty-nine days after death. It is strongly encouraged to arrange this ahead of time as well as plan financially to make the offerings, and include this information in your Dharma Will. By doing so, the prayers can be recited at the most beneficial time and someone else does not need to make arrangements in the midst of a difficult situation.

Appendix III offers a sample Dharma Will, but here I'll address in general what kinds of things might well be covered by the document.

Considerations for a Dharma Will

The Dharma Will should include instructions for our entrusted Dharma friends and for non-Buddhist family and friends, and requests concerning prayers and ceremonies at our burial or cremation (see addendums in Appendix III).

If we do not actually write these documents in a timely manner, give them to our family and entrusted Dharma friends, and place extra copies in our Dharma Box, we risk losing precious opportunities for liberation when we die. We will not be able to take advantage of the fruition of our practice.

It is helpful to take time now to call or visit local funeral homes or crematoriums and discuss our special requests with them. Some are more accommodating to Buddhist traditions than others—especially the practice of not moving or disturbing the body for several days after death. Ideally we should know which places would be best ahead of time. When we do this, we can include their names and contact information for our family and entrusted Dharma friends.

I have been happy to hear stories of practitioners who were allowed to keep the body of their loved one at home for the traditional three days after death. Family members and the lama were able to pray and do phowa; then they were also allowed to be at the cremation to continue praying. This gave the family great confidence that the deceased practitioner had received all the blessings needed to support them in their journey in the bardo states.

Another student told me about organizations that help people bring a loved one home from the hospital, nursing home, or hospice after death, conduct a funeral at home, and then transport the body to the crematorium or burial site after three days. The names and websites of several of these organizations can be found in Appendix IV. If we decide to make such arrangements, we must discuss this ahead of time to be sure non-Buddhist family members understand why we have requested this and that they are in agreement with this wish to be taken home for three days.

Arrangements should be made in advance so that the details have been taken care of and the health care staff is or can be advised. We must be aware of any legalities surrounding after-death care and we must choose a designated person to take care of these details.

Truly, it is most important that we discuss our *entire* Dharma Will not only with entrusted Dharma friends but with our family members as well. It is imperative that we help our loved ones understand our spiritual goals while, at the same time, respecting their feelings and beliefs.

I want to emphasize here that we must focus on true Dharma and not become too attached to certain traditions. We should not fall into any extremes. While it is good to make a plan for what to do with the body after death, we should remember that once the consciousness has left the physical body, the body is no longer useful. We may be very attached to our bodies, but we cannot recycle them! Realized masters have no attachment to the physical body and are not concerned with what happens to it after they die.

The body has served its purpose and we should let go of any attachment to it, turning our attention wholly to the Dharma.

Practicing Generosity in Preparation for Death

In the Tibetan Buddhist tradition, practitioners who know they are going to die distribute their wealth to friends and family beforehand. This can actually be beneficial to avoid any arguments among family members. But regardless of whether we choose to distribute any wealth we have acquired before our death or after, we should also decide ahead of time what kinds of activities we wish to support. We may wish to support schools, nunneries, retreatants, or other Dharma organizations. But also, we should practice generosity for any positive activity that we feel inspired to contribute to. After all, this is the very last action we will take, and the last karma we will accrue, based on our activities of this lifetime! We should take some time to consider these last acts of charity.

We have worked hard during our lives. At the time of death, we should do something not only for our own benefit, but for all beings who will be in the bardos when we die. Requesting prayers and practices to help liberate beings in the bardo states is a meritorious act that will go with us on our journey.

5

THE DHARMA BOX

THE DHARMA BOX contains all the items we and our entrusted Dharma friends will need to help us actualize our Dharma Vision and carry out our Dharma Will at the time of death. It will take some commitment and diligence to complete our preparation of the Dharma Box; we need to be thorough and include each practice and prayer we wish to have recited, as well as all ritual items upon which we wish to rely. We will once more benefit by envisioning our own ideal deaths, "hearing" our most familiar practices being read to us, and thinking about what photos, thangkas, and statues inspire us the most.

Putting together our Dharma Box is an excellent endeavor that allows us to continue reviewing our spiritual progress. Many of my students found that they had forgotten various oral instructions and practices; by reviewing and consolidating their notes as they planned for death, they were able to reinvigorate their current practice. And this personal text can serve as a constant reminder of what our teachers have instructed us to practice. The scriptures remind us of the many aspects of devotion and generosity that we can use to repay our spiritual teachers—the greatest being putting their teachings into practice. Without this vigilant self-reflection on our own progress, the jewels we have been offered by our teachers become encrusted by layers of dirt that will later take great effort to unearth. It is best to keep these jewels polished and offer them back tenfold!

By the conclusion of this book, we will know the most important practices to focus on at the time of death and what written materials to gather. If death does not arrive before our annual review of the Dharma Will, we can certainly add anything meaningful to our Dharma Box at that time. Thus, we can aspire to remain constantly mindful of our practices; our progress; the teachings that help us increase our devotion, faith, and bodhichitta; and awareness and preparation for the always-approaching moment of death.

I encourage you to set a time for completing the Dharma Box quickly and then communicate with family and entrusted Dharma friends about its contents and where it is being kept. Again, I suggest those participating in a core group of entrusted Dharma friends come together to train, listen to each other's Dharma Visions and Wills, and become familiar with what is in each person's Dharma Box.

Students who have been working on their Dharma Boxes suggest having a three-ring binder or something similar for each entrusted Dharma friend that holds all the practices we wish them to recite. All instructions for entrusted Dharma friends and family members should be organized, easy to find, and clear. Some students have given the binders to their entrusted Dharma friends as soon as they were completed, but they have also put one or two extra binders in the Dharma Box as well. If entrusted Dharma friends keep binders with them at home, they should ensure that they are kept confidential.

We should have a separate binder or file with copies of any general Tibetan Buddhist prayers we find meaningful. Non-Buddhist family and friends are welcome to recite them, but should also be encouraged to use whatever is familiar to them from their own traditions if that is more comfortable for them.

A Checklist for Dharma Box Contents

☐ A copy of all legal papers (wills, medical directives, etc.)

☐ A copy of the Dharma Will

☐ Instructions to entrusted Dharma friends

☐ Instructions to non-Buddhist family members

☐ Binders with copies for ourselves and designated entrusted Dharma friends that include:

    ☐ Our daily practice(s) including refuge and bodhisattva vows

    ☐ Yidam practice

    ☐ Phowa text

    ☐ Oral instructions received from our lama (see chapter 15 for instructions on who may read this to you)

    ☐ Any other prayers we wish to be recited

    ☐ Dedication prayers

☐ Binders with copies of general prayers for non-Buddhist family and friends

☐ Framed or laminated photos of spiritual guides and deities, and statues and ritual items for the bedside altar (there are some "traveling altars" that stand on their own and may be useful)

☐ A photo of yourself kneeling and praying with palms together if you wish to have a lama perform phowa or chod for you. (*Chod* is the tantric practice of cutting through self-attachment in which we visualize our body as an offering to satisfy the needs, desires, and negative karma of all beings, and is a very useful practice at the time of death, especially if the deceased is a young person who has died in an accident.) If you have previously arranged for this, the photo can be sent ahead to your lama.

☐ *Dutsi,* or blessed pills

☐ An extra mala in case your regular mala is not with you

☐ Tea lights, candle holder, incense and incense holder if we wish

(entrusted Dharma friends should consider any respiratory issues for us and anyone else who could be affected, as well as whether it is permitted in our environment)

☐ Recordings of phowa, mantras, and other recitations

☐ The means to play this recording, along with a set of earphones if you wish, or an agreement with entrusted Dharma friends or family to have this available

☐ A liberation-by-wearing (Tib. *tagdrol*) mandala (see chapter 13 for more information on these)

Items such as dutsi and tagdrol mandalas can be obtained from your lama, from monasteries, or from the Phowa Foundation.

Make the time in your life now to complete the important work of carefully creating your Dharma Box. You will feel very fortunate to have done so at the time of death and will inspire others to do the same. Your confidence to die will be greatly increased as you continue your commitment to work diligently on the path and prepare for death.

PART TWO

—m—

Spiritual Practices
as the Time of Death Nears

6

THE BARDOS OF LIVING AND DYING

BUDDHISM DESCRIBES the cycle of birth, death, and rebirth as a series of transitional or intermediate states called *bardos*. Many people have read or at least heard of "The Tibetan Book of the Dead," which is used to guide a dying person and describes in detail the experiences of the after-death states. Our current human existence is also considered a bardo, the Bardo of Birth and Living. It, too, is a transitional state and cannot last forever.

There are excellent books and translations of texts now available in the West that describe the various bardo states and what we may expect to happen after our death. Still, we may have some confusion about what practices to do and the appropriate times to do them, so I will give brief teachings here to help Buddhist practitioners prepare for death. These will also be useful for those assisting others through the dying process. Once more, for Buddhists, I emphasize the importance of daily practice so that the bardo states can become opportunities for liberation. Non-Buddhists may use these teachings to become familiar with the Buddhist view of death and need not be concerned about the details.

Teachings on the bardos are so profound that it is important we receive further instruction on them directly from our spiritual teacher. These teachings instruct us in life-long practices that we need to hear repeatedly until we are confident in our understanding and preparations.

To approach death in the best possible way, we need three supports for our practice during the Bardo of Birth and Living. First is to meet with an excellent lama. Secondly, we need to study intensively and receive profound instructions from that lama. Thirdly, we need to keep the *samaya*, the sacred conduct, of the lineage purely. If we are not familiar with what samaya is, and especially the five root samayas of the Secret Mantrayana, we should consult with our lama and ask for teachings so that we can be clear what conduct we are to keep when we receive certain lineage teachings. But we could say, in the most general way, that if we uphold or repair the virtuous mind of bodhichitta in every situation, that we are keeping the supreme samaya. (A very condensed teaching on the five root samayas can be found in Appendix VI.) It is said in the Buddhist scriptures that if we have these three supports, illness and death will be of no consequence. These three things are essential supports for dying with confidence.

The texts generally talk about six bardo states; however, the Bardo of Birth and Living includes those of Dreaming and of Meditative Concentration, so the six are condensed into four. We will only briefly mention the Bardo of Birth and Living as we have already discussed the most effective practices for this bardo when we reflected on the Dharma Vision. The essential preparations for the time of our death and the after-death bardo states are honest self-reflection and the diligent practice of mindfulness and meditation as we have been instructed by a close spiritual teacher. We should objectively assess our current practice and our experience of the essential meaning of the teachings. The great majority of us do not have the truly excellent capacity to attain liberation before we reach the after-death bardos. So it is of utmost importance to be prepared for the experiences of the bardos and to train now to recognize them as expressions of our own mind that could be recognized as the display of wisdom.

The Bardo of Birth and Living

The Bardo of Birth and Living lasts from the moment of birth until the moment of death. Each bardo is represented metaphorically in the teachings; the metaphor for this bardo is of a hawk who finds the perfect place to build a nest. When the hawk dives into the nest, it is free of doubt and completely fearless. We practitioners should follow this example in our practice and learn to be confident and fearless of whatever seeming dangers present themselves.

The Dream Bardo is contained within this bardo; we all spend time in the dream state each night. The metaphor for the Dream Bardo is a candle that lights a dark room and dispels the darkness of ignorance. This represents learning to become aware while we are dreaming and becoming able to meditate in that state.

The Bardo of Meditative Concentration is all-pervasive; it actually applies to all bardos. We enter this bardo when the mind expresses the instantaneous self-liberation of any concept that arises. The metaphor is that of a beautiful woman looking in a mirror. As soon as the condition of the mirror being held before her face arises, the image appears. In just that same way, as soon as the mind comes into contact with any concept, it is liberated.

If we have not yet received teachings on self-liberating concepts, we can explore what it means to rest in the view by doing preparatory practices such as *ngondro* or reflecting on the Four Mind Turnings and seeking instruction from a qualified lama; or when thoughts arise, we can simply let them be and not grasp at them or push them away. We do not have to be rigid and practice only in one way. Experience is gained by trying different things and trying to understand what the words of the teachings actually mean in conjunction with serious and applied study with a qualified lama. A qualified lama not only has deep experience in the practices of self-liberation, but that lama is also capable of sharing such experiences with a student if the student is qualified to receive such instruction.

The Bardo of Dying

The metaphor in the texts for the Bardo of Dying is a king's seal or, in modern terms, a travel visa. Just as we can go anywhere with a visa, we can use the supreme technique of phowa in this bardo to bring ourselves to a favorable rebirth or to attain complete liberation, as long as we know the appropriate time to practice as the signs of death are appearing.

We all know that we must die; it is a logical consequence of taking birth. And we know that, at the time of our death, we are incapable of taking our wealth or possessions or even the people we love and cherish the most. When we contemplate the experience of losing loved ones and material wealth, we need an indestructible kind of meditation to help us through the overwhelming suffering of death.

Longchenpa, the great Tibetan master who revealed the Longchen Nyingthig cycle of the Dzogchen teachings, wrote about this indestructible kind of meditation in the fourteenth century. He said that a yogi must seriously examine the origin of the arising of fear, where fear abides, and where it ceases, in order to be completely free from the fear of death. When we examine the place of arising, abiding, and cessation of fear (or any afflictive emotion) and cannot find them, we should rest in the confidence that all phenomena are beyond arising, abiding, and cessation. This helps us to gain an intellectual and intuitive sense of the empty nature of all phenomena, and gives us the sense of their ultimate nature. However, it can only truly become a living experience when the student relies upon a qualified lama who directly introduces that student to the nature of mind. Then when we, skillful yogis endowed with certainty in the practice of meditation, reach the Bardo of Dying, we will have fearless confidence.

7

THE SIGNS OF DEATH

WHEN I WAS LIVING in Tibet, I witnessed the deaths of hundreds of people. I was present with them and watched them die. Although not everyone had all the signs of death we will discuss, there was no one who did not manifest some of them. Each of us, if mindful and present during the process of dying, can use the signs of death to further our progress on the spiritual path.

To fulfill our Dharma Visions, we must know the signs of approaching death intimately; they are the keys to using our practice in the most beneficial way. Generally, Western students have little exposure to the process of dying, but with this knowledge and sufficient training in mindfulness to recognize the signs *as they are happening,* our preparations for death will bear the fruit we are seeking. Everyone who wishes to be an entrusted Dharma friend for another person must know these signs well so that precious opportunities will not be lost.

The Dying Process and the Stages of Dissolution

Untrained individuals and Buddhist practitioners with little experience will find the transitions in the bardo states to be almost instantaneous and unrecognizable; for those with greater training, the experiences of the bardo states will vary according to the individual's ability to abide in the view. The important thing is that we need to recognize the signs, apply our daily practice, and attempt to abide in the view during the dissolution process in order to achieve liberation.

Dissolution is traditionally classified into many stages, but here I will give a condensed summary of three major stages for us to reflect upon. The first is the dissolution of the sense faculties; the second is the dissolution of the elements; and the third is the continuum of appearance, increase, attainment, and full attainment.

Again, more detailed instruction than I can give here should be obtained by cultivating a close relationship with an authentic spiritual friend and receiving oral or *upadesha* instructions on the teachings of the great masters. It is important to note that, if we are experienced practitioners, we should be ready to practice whatever oral instructions we have been given as the stages of dissolution begin.

The Dissolution of the Senses

In terms of the five sense faculties, many of us will find that the signs of "far-away" death have already occurred. We notice that our hearing and vision are not as clear as they used to be, and our body has lost some of its flexibility and strength. As death comes closer, the degradation of the five faculties is more marked. One thing to be mindful of as we train in the signs of approaching death: we should not become too attached to the idea that one sense faculty always degrades first; it may vary from person to person.

The first faculty that usually dissolves when death is imminent is that of hearing. At this stage we will be unable to clearly hear sounds

or voices. In Tibet, this would usually be the sound of lamas praying around the dying person. We may need to ask for things to be
repeated, or we may hear sounds but be unable to understand what
they mean. All of these are signs that the ear faculty is dissolving.

Two things should happen at this time. We, ourselves, should
recognize that our hearing is deteriorating and bring to mind any
instructions or profound teachings that we have been given by our
root lama. Additionally, our entrusted Dharma friends should recognize this as a sign of dying and remind us to begin practicing. At
this time, the entrusted Dharma friends begin to act as supports to
our mindfulness.

This would also be an appropriate time to invite our lama to be
present if possible and for he or she to give us the introduction to
the nature of mind or remind us of any critical instructions previously given.

The next faculty that typically dissolves is the faculty of the eyes.
Our eyesight may be blurry, and we may not recognize the faces of
friends and family. The dissolution of the remaining sense faculties
would be recognized as the inability for us to smell; the inability to
taste food; and the inability of our body to sense it is being touched.
After one sense faculty begins to deteriorate, the others will follow
one after another.

It is most important to recognize the beginning of this series
of dissolutions while the capacity to practice is still strong. Our
entrusted Dharma friends should recognize any loss of the sense
faculties as the time to begin reading our daily and yidam practices.
If we are experienced with phowa, this would be the time to begin
practicing.

We can have hope, then, that when we die, our daily practice will
actually benefit us. If we cannot remember it ourselves, or at the
time of death no one is there to remind us, we can die in an almost

unconscious state. In that condition, we will not be able to remember to use these practices while we are dying.

The possibility of dying in such a way should point out how crucial mindfulness training is during our lifetime when we are strong and healthy. As the sense faculties dissolve, we must be able to rely upon mindfulness. It is the time to remember our lama or, for non-Buddhists, any essential person we have relied upon spiritually or any inspiration or teaching of compassion we have received.

The Dissolution of the Elements

The following description of how the elements dissolve is more familiar to us in Tibet and in other countries where it is common to die at home and without medication. For centuries, these observations were accurate and I believe they remain useful even today.

There is no certainty about when the dissolution of the elements will begin. The teachings present them as if the five sense faculties will dissolve first and then the elements. But when we work with people who are dying we sometimes see that these are occurring simultaneously. As such, we must train in general mindfulness of all of the signs and so hope to become aware of when the elements begin to dissolve. If our entrusted Dharma friends are able to do this, they will be able to guide us well through these stages and remind us of our focus.

We should know that it is not only at the time of death that the elements can be found in an unbalanced state; we can become ill when any element is out of balance. Understanding this, we can influence both our physical and mental health by learning how to bring our elements into balance. When the earth element is too strong, for example, we may experience depression, a lack of diligence, sleepiness, or laziness. When our fire element becomes too strong, we may experience an illness that manifests through heat, perhaps a fever or an illness associated with the liver. If our wind element is too high, it can manifest as anxiety and sometimes as a chronic mental illness like bipolar disorder.

I have included here a short explanation on how the elements and energy in the body interact with one another when we are still living, and then as we are dying. I think many students will find that this is helpful in understanding why the Bardo of Dying is a supreme opportunity for realization and liberation.

Generally speaking, the elements are separate when our bodies are functioning properly. The elements are in perfect balance within the body, which allows energy to move freely. Although wind, which carries energy, is considered a separate element, it is also contained in earth, water, and fire. It is the element that helps keep the body's functions working properly.

Briefly, there are five major types of wind energy: upward-moving wind; downward-cleansing wind; heat; all-pervasive energy; and the life-upholding wind. When the energy of one element is cut off, the element becomes charged with energy and the agitation causes the impure aspect of that element to dissolve. As a result, we experience the expression of that element dissolving.

We can receive teachings from our lama about the dissolution of the elements that go into great depth and detail. Here it is enough for us to understand that when we talk about the dissolution of the elements during the dying process, we are talking about the dissolution of each element's impure aspect, which leaves its pure wisdom aspect behind. Thus, when an element dissolves, we have an enhanced capacity to abide in or experience the nature of mind. This is due to the increased pure energy, or "wisdom wind" in the central channel as each element is purified.

Simultaneously, changes are occurring in the physical organs of the body. We will discuss these as well to understand the outer signs that manifest as the body loses its ability to maintain life.

The Earth Element, or Flesh, Dissolves into the Water Element

Earth will be the first element to dissolve. While we will say more about the "channels" a little later, right now it is important to know that, as each element dissolves, a knot in the channels loosens and becomes "untied," which allows energy to flow through them. The energy in the element which is dissolving becomes agitated. This separates the pure from the impure aspects of the element, and allows the pure aspects to manifest fully. The dissolution of the earth element, for instance, begins with the knot at the navel coming untied. The dissolution causes us to experience its physical expression: the heaviness of the body and a degradation in physical strength. We typically feel that we are falling into a very deep hole or as though we are being pinned down by an entire mountain. We may ask someone to help pull us up or make our pillow higher to counteract the feeling of being pulled down. This is an outer sign that we and our entrusted Dharma friends should recognize.

At this time, the blood flow to the spleen is cut off. From the Tibetan Buddhist point of view, as well as in Chinese medicine, the spleen is considered the earth center and the source of the body's *chi*, or energy, and blood. The spleen is said to be responsible for keeping the blood contained within the blood vessels, just as the earth forms riverbeds and shores to keep water contained. Without blood circulating through the spleen, the earth element in the body begins to dissolve into the water element. This is when the body begins to feel heavy.

Kindle mindfulness at this time and recognize that "I am experiencing the process of death." The entrusted Dharma friend also needs to help the dying person by expressing this out loud.

Consider this passage from Tsasum Lingpa's *Peaceful and Wrathful Liberation Upon Hearing* (translated by Allison Graboski).

When the earth element dissolves into water,
The illusory body feels heavy and tortured [by being] pressed down.
The earth element, the spleen channel, is cut off and the earth's wind energy is agitated.
The thunderous cracking of the destruction of great mountains sounds.
Vidyadhara Lama, draw me out through the strength of your compassion.
After remembering the introduction to intrinsic, primordial awareness,
May I recognize the bardo as the face of my own [mind].

The Water Element, or Blood, Dissolves into the Fire Element

This dissolution begins when the knot at the heart center comes untied. The branch channels that connect the kidneys to the other bodily systems are cut off. The kidneys govern water, so we will feel the need to expel liquid from the body quickly, even if we are unable to do so. Liquid will leak from the mouth and nose and we will feel very thirsty. With some people, steam can actually be seen coming off the top of the head. The kidneys also store the essential *chi* in the body. With the kidneys unable to function, the body can no longer accumulate the energy needed to maintain life.

Again, reflect on the words of Tsasum Lingpa:

When the water element dissolves into fire,
The mind buzzes; the mouth and nose are dry and [cannot
  draw in air].
The water element, the kidney channel, is cut off and the
  water's wind energy is agitated.
The crashing of great ocean waves appears.
Vidyadhara Lama, draw me out through the strength of your
  compassion.
After remembering the introduction to intrinsic, primordial
  awareness,
May I recognize the bardo as the face of my own [mind].

The Fire Element, or Warmth, Dissolves into the Wind Element

As the knot in the throat area comes untied, the energy of the fire element becomes agitated. The impure aspect of fire dissolves and its pure wisdom aspect enters the central channel. Physically, our breathing pattern is affected and we are no longer able to speak. The liver's connection to the other bodily systems is cut off and, with its energy impeded, the blood vessels cannot remain open. The blood flow diminishes and the body's warmth begins to dissipate.

The warmth of the body will gather and move out of the body from one end to the other. It may start at the feet and move to the top of the head or vice-versa. It is said that for someone who has not gathered the two accumulations of wisdom and merit, developed bodhichitta, and trained in the experience of primordial wisdom, the heat will gather in the head, move to the toes, and leave the body through the bottoms of the feet. For someone who has trained in these, the heat will move from the feet upward and leave the body through the top of the head.

Tsasum Lingpa says:

When the element of fire dissolves into wind,
Breath is shallow and words [are unclear], the eyes roll up.
The fire element, the liver channel, is cut and the fire's wind
    energy is agitated.
The roar of fire sounds.
Vidyadhara Lama, draw me out through the strength of your
    compassion.
After remembering the introduction to intrinsic, primordial
    awareness,
May I recognize the bardo as the face of my own [mind].

The Wind Element, or Breath, Dissolves into Consciousness

At this point in the dying process, the knot at the secret area below
the navel loosens and comes untied. The place of the breath's natural abiding, the lungs, is cut off from the rest of the body and the
breath becomes agitated. The lungs are considered the "master" of
the body's energy, or chi. They sit at the top of the body's main cavity
and are connected to the throat above and the heart and liver below.
All bodily chi is said to have its physical origin in the lungs, which
then transport the energy to the other organs. Once the connections
to the lungs are cut off, the "coarse" or physical breath is interrupted
and we are not able to breathe. The oxygen-deficient blood then
flows into the heart.

On a subtle level, the first four wind energies are dissolving into
the life-upholding wind, the breath that keeps us alive. The mixing
of the different wind energies in the body causes the impure wind
aspect to dissolve and the pure aspect to enter into what is called
the five-colored lifeforce channel. When it enters this channel, the
relationship between the coarse physical breath and the subtle wind
energy is severed.

It is said in the scriptures that the blood then pulses into our heart three times and we exhale three times, but we are no longer able to inhale. At this point our "outer breath" ceases.

When I was in Tibet with my uncle, who is a great chod practitioner, I conducted a rather unscientific experiment. Chod is a tantric practice in which one makes one's own body an offering to satisfy the needs and desires of all beings, and to overcome attachment, self-clinging and negative karma. Chod practitioners in Tibet perform sky burials; they cut up bodies and offer them to vultures. When I went with my uncle to do this, I would examine the bodies. I wanted to find out if they were going to bleed or not, because according to the teachings, the blood should have been drawn into the heart and they should not bleed. In fact, I found that dead bodies do not bleed. A little blood may come from the flesh, but when you think about how much blood is actually in a person's body, they really do not bleed.

Let's turn to one last passage from Tsasum Lingpa:

> When the element of wind dissolves into the consciousness,
> Warmth condenses and outer appearances set.
> The wind element, the lung channel, is cut off and the wind
>   energy is agitated.
> A sound like a dragon's roar resounds.
> Vidyadhara Lama, draw me out through the strength of your
>   compassion.
> May the realization of profound wisdom completely manifest
> [and] may I recognize the bardo as the face of my own [mind].

When wind dissolves into consciousness, we are close to the moment of death, but according to Buddhist texts we are not actually dead until the "inner breath" ceases. The Bardo of Dying is not yet complete. This time, when the outer breath has ceased and before the inner breath ceases, is one of the most beneficial times for a lama to be present.

It is very difficult for a dying person to recognize the moment when the outer breath ceases; we need knowledgeable entrusted Dharma friends, and our lama if possible, as well as incredible mindfulness at this time. Yet if we practice now, it will definitely benefit us!

In the West, the signs of the dissolution of the elements may be difficult to notice if life-support technology takes over some of the dying person's bodily functions. If we are practitioners with strong faith in Dharma and we believe that we are dying, we may want to decide in advance about using life support when we are at this advanced stage in the dying process, leaving advance directives to inform friends, family, and physicians about our wishes. This is, of course, a very emotional decision for the friends and family of the person who is dying, and one that is difficult to make when the process of death has actually begun. I believe that each and every being should have the right to make these decisions for themselves and to die as they wish.

The Cessation of the Inner Breath

After the dissolution of the elements culminates in the cessation of the outer breath, then comes the cessation of the inner breath. Four stages lead up to this: the stages of appearance, increase, attainment, and full attainment. We'll explore each of them below in order. As these stages progress from one to another, the male and female energies that reside in their respective white ("Lunar") and red ("Solar") bodily channels must be purified and moved into the central channel. For an ordinary practitioner, this will take around three days. For a great practitioner or master who can abide for long periods of time in meditative concentration, the inner breath will not cease for perhaps one or two weeks.

The Stage of Appearance

The dissolution of the wind element causes the purified white, male essence to begin moving downward from the crown of the head toward the heart. At this time, we will see a very vast and perfectly pure sky lit up by a halo of white light, as though there were a very bright moon in the sky. Everything we see is of that pure white color—first the vast sky and the halo of white light and then everything turns completely white. The moon is symbolic of the male consort or masculine energy; the white light is the expression of the perfectly pure self-radiance of the consciousness. This stage is named *appearance* because the self-radiance of the consciousness is naturally able to appear.

The inner sign of this stage is the manifestation of the "wisdom of appearance," which is an experience of uncommon mental clarity free of any concepts. The mind itself is filled with clear white light. It is not a sense of the body *filling with* light—this light is the experience of clear awareness. When we are alive, the mind is said to "ride the wind energy," which puts the mind in motion and creates the arising of concepts. Now that the wind energy has dissolved, the mind's motion ceases, along with conceptual thought and memory. All anger has ceased as well. This state of clear awareness, along with the absence of anger, is called the *luminosity of appearance* or *empty luminosity*.

The vision of white light and this experience of inner clarity can be so beautiful we might feel attachment or craving toward it, but it is important to recognize that this experience of light is not the same as liberation. This can be a particular problem for Western students, who frequently hear in their culture that we should "go into" the light. Attachment to this light will become cause for rebirth in samsara. Dzogchen practice enables us to cut through the attachment that is likely to arise (it is important to have received instruction beforehand from an experienced, qualified teacher). At this point, it would be very helpful for an entrusted Dharma friend to whisper in our ear, "Remember, no matter what appearances arise in your mind, do not become attached to them."

The Stage of Increase

The red, female essence from the mother is purified of attachment and ascends the central channel from the navel toward the heart. The sun is symbolic of feminine energy, and the outer sign of this stage is the sky at dawn tinged with beautiful red. The inner sign at this stage is called "the wisdom of increase" and is a feeling of bliss indivisible from clear awareness. This experience is called the *luminosity of increase.*

As sentient beings we are extremely habituated to attachment. Even though in this particular stage of dying the poison of attachment naturally dissolves, we can still generate attachment to this experience. So if we have any mindfulness whatsoever at this point, it is important for us to cut through our attachment to the experience of bliss and clarity that arises at this stage. We can prepare for this every day by, for instance, enjoying without attachment the beauty of a sunrise.

The Stage of Attainment

The pure aspects of the male and female have now moved through the central channel, the white essence descending and the red essence ascending. When they meet in the heart center, they cover the consciousness. The life-upholding wind as well as the channels to the heart are now cut off; the blood can no longer move out of the heart and we "faint." All outer appearances turn black.

This stage is called the *luminosity of attainment*. The inner sign, called "the wisdom of attainment," is a heightened experience of indivisible bliss and clarity that is free of any concept or thought. This is the natural ceasing of bewilderment, symbolized by fogginess or darkness—the origin from which ignorance can arise is no longer present. We should cut through any aversion to the darkness of this stage with effortless mindfulness.

At this time, the five subtle gates of sensory consciousnesses— the five organs that enable us to see, hear, smell, taste, and feel— dissolve. Non-conceptual mind dissolves into the expanse, free of sensory feeling, and we abide in cessation. Additionally, the texts of many masters say that dissolution of consciousness into space has occurred at this point.

The Stage of Full Attainment

If we have received an introduction to the nature of mind and have trained extensively, we will awaken from the experience of darkness and fainting to the naked experience of a perfectly pure sky, the clear cloudless sky of autumn, completely non-dual and free of concepts. This is the *ground luminosity*, and it is free of limitations, and of any characteristics that give it shape or dimension. As the experience is completely stainless, this stage is called *full attainment*. This is the nature of Dharmakaya, and if we recognize it and are able to rest in it free of any contrivance, we may realize the vast expanse of the Dharmakaya and attain liberation.

The ground luminosity appears to all beings going through the process of dying, but if we have not received an introduction to the nature of mind, instructions on how to abide in the nature of mind, and trained in that extensively during our lifetimes, the appearance of ground luminosity will be instantaneous and unrecognizable. At this point, the inner breath ceases.

It is uncertain how long the appearance of the ground luminosity will last for an experienced practitioner. Scriptures say it will last about as long as it takes to eat a meal (note that in Tibet, that is not a very long time!). There are many practices that we can train in during our lives to make the appearance of the ground luminosity more stable: *tsa lung,* or yantra yoga; practices of the channels, energies, and essences; habituation to abiding in the view itself; experience in meditation; and having a stable *shamatha,* or *calm-abiding,* practice. These techniques and experiences enable us to abide in this state longer.

To understand such a profound idea as the ground luminosity, we should take time to study texts like the *Uttaratantra,* Mipham Rinpoche's *Beacon of Certainty,* and also the logic of Madhyamika, the Middle Way philosophy founded by Nagarjuna. In these texts, buddha-nature, the primordially pure enlightened essence, is described and defined in great detail. Based on these studies, we will be able to understand how the expression and recognition of the naked Dharmakaya are possible. If we are to really strive to put these teachings into practice, it is most important that we gain true experience and don't just take the teachings at face value. In terms of the experience of the ground luminosity, merely talking about receiving such teachings does not help us to recognize that experience—not even a little bit.

Liberation is easier, of course, during this state because the three poisons of anger, desire, and bewilderment have naturally ceased. During our human existence, we have to work hard to purify our afflictive emotions. However, at the moment of this particular experience, they naturally dissolve; if we have trained well, our practice will be powerful and we will attain results.

Again, it is important to recognize that our ability to practice in the moment of the ground luminosity totally depends on our lifelong practice and our prior training in mindfulness and discernment. This should help us think about the kind of practice we need to have over our lifetime in order to recognize this moment and whether we can make that kind of commitment to practice in our Dharma Vision. We can at least aspire to become this kind of practitioner and to receive teachings that will lead us to this ability.

We should also aspire to train with an authentic and experienced teacher on the practices of cutting through—*rangdrol, cherdrol,* and *shardrol* in Tibetan—so that we are able to rest undistractedly in the natural state at the time of death.

8

LIBERATION IN THE BARDOS AFTER DEATH

LET ME FIRST answer a question that often arises in students' minds: "How is it that someone knew the experiences of the bardo states after death and wrote them down in so much detail?" The answer is that there is a tradition of uncommon yogis called *delogs*, those who "come-and-go" between life and death. These are beings who are said to die completely and remain dead for at least a week or two. They are able to enter other realms, other states, and then come back to life. These yogis, as well as some omniscient practitioners like Padmasambhava, have described each stage of the bardo in great detail. Their writings have evolved into the tradition of bardo teachings and preparation for the experience of death through meditation.

One of my root teachers, Dorlo Rinpoche, was just such a delog in a past incarnation. He wrote a book about his experiences after he died and went to benefit beings in another realm. Almost all of what he wrote could be straight from the bardo commentaries.

I will not go into as much detail here as the delogs have done, as many accounts of their journeys into the bardo states are available in the West. And you will find detailed descriptions of the appearances of the Bardo of Suchness in texts such as *The Tibetan Book of the Dead*. Here, I will again give a condensed version of teachings that will hopefully motivate us not only to study more with an authentic lama, but to practice with great diligence and focus!

Attaining Fearless Confidence

To have fearless confidence upon which we can rely in the Bardo of Suchness, we must have practiced diligently in the Bardo of Birth and Living. We cannot naively think that meditative stability will somehow be naturally possible in this bardo. That is a fantasy we should abandon.

If we really have fearless confidence along with a lifetime of diligent training in the luminosity of the path, we would be able to recognize the ground luminosity as the mind's true nature in its first instant of appearance in the Bardo of Dying. The lack of such confidence is one of the factors that can cause us to enter the Bardo of Suchness. Just as a reminder, it becomes more and more difficult to recognize opportunities for liberation the deeper we go into the bardo states.

One way to practice fearlessness in the bardos is in our dreams. Students sometimes tell me that they have experienced in their dreams some of the phenomena of the Bardo of Dying or the Bardo of Suchness, and become frightened that they were going to die. As we fall asleep, our five senses are being cut off in just the same way as when we die. We can infer from our experiences in the Dream Bardo what the after-death bardo state would be like. If you are a great practitioner of Dzogchen, this is a great time to practice. If you are not a great practitioner of Dzogchen, then generate loving-kindness and compassion to help stabilize your mind.

When I was young I went alone to a part of Tibet which was said to be haunted by ghosts. I did chod practice, went to sleep, and had some terrible dreams. In my dreams, I tried to visualize myself as

Vajrakilaya and become very wrathful. The dreams became worse. Then I remembered my root lama's advice, that bodhichitta is the most powerful practice one can do. I did tonglen and compassion practices and my dreams became very positive!

The Bardo of Suchness

As a general note, the teachings of great masters sometimes explain the exact moment when the Bardo of Suchness begins and the inner breath ceases with slight distinctions. These experiences are occurring very quickly—perhaps there is only a moment between one stage and the next. If you do extensive reading on this subject, please do not see these explanations as contradictory. They are related to that particular master's experience as it unfolded.

If we cannot recognize the first instant of the ground luminosity in the Bardo of Dying and attain liberation, we will enter the Bardo of Suchness. To achieve liberation in the Bardo of Dying, one must have superior faculties. However, even a practitioner of middle capacity can master the Bardo of Suchness, the expression of the Sambhogakaya.

At this point, our consciousness has gone through a transformation; it no longer resembles our afflicted or conceptual consciousness. Wisdom is all that remains. It is as though our ordinary consciousness has dissolved into something vast like the sky. This gives us a great opportunity for practice. Thus, there are many profound instructions for this bardo that we should aspire to receive from our lama.

In the Bardo of Dying, the manifestation of the Dharmakaya was based on the strength of the four luminosities in the stages of appearance, increase, attainment, and full attainment. To gain liberation in the Bardo of Suchness, we must recognize all appearances as expressions of our own mind. In order to do this, we must have elicited the perfectly pure meaning of the instructions we have received and practiced them exactly as they were taught. Then we can experience the appearances of the Bardo of Suchness completely free of fear and know they are the play of wisdom. Based on this understanding, we once more have an opportunity to attain liberation.

In this state where all sense faculties and elements have dissolved, all phenomena are empty and vast like the sky. The metaphor for the Bardo of Suchness is the union of Samantabhadhri, the aspect of emptiness, with Samantabhadra, the aspect of clarity. At the first moment of "awakening" to this bardo, we once again experience the ground luminosity that we were unable to recognize in the last moments of the Bardo of Dying. If a lama is present with us at this time, he or she would whisper over and over again the instructions to abide in the indivisibility of clarity and emptiness.

Should we recognize this luminosity now as the mind's true nature, we will be liberated instantly and complete our journey in the bardo states. If not, we will have more opportunities, but as we progress further into the bardo state they become more difficult to recognize.

The Luminosities of the Bardo of Suchness

Expressions of wisdom appear in this bardo because we are now free of the eight kinds of ordinary consciousnesses; the reliance of the consciousnesses upon sense objects no longer exists. Thus, the pure aspects of the five *skandhas*—of form, feeling, perception, karmic formations, and consciousness—become all-pervasive. Our inherently present buddha-nature is a natural attribute; therefore any expression of this as sacred sound, buddha realms, deities, etc.

must also be inherently present as a natural attribute. Thus the mind's perfectly pure five qualities of wisdom are expressed.

Although we experience the sounds, lights, and images ("forms") of this bardo in stages, they are actually appearing at the same time. Without great mindfulness at this point and without understanding these phenomena as expressions of the mind's awareness, we will feel great fear. We will experience all the appearances as if they were outside of us.

In the bardos, there is a constant tendency of the untrained mind to generate either fear or attachment. First we experience something we find unpleasant, and then suddenly there is something we experience as very pleasant. We must recognize the sounds, lights, and forms as expressions of wisdom and we must avoid generating attachment or aversion toward any of them. If we generate attachment, we will go on to take rebirth in one of the six realms of sentient beings—the hell realms, the realm of hungry ghosts, the animal realms, the human realm, the realm of jealous gods, or the god realms—rather than achieve liberation here in the bardo.

The Five Days of Meditative Concentration

During the Bardo of Suchness, we will experience what is called the *five days of meditative concentration*. Each "day" corresponds to the appearance of one of the Five Wisdom Buddhas—Vairochana, Akshobhya, Ratnasambhava, Amitabha, and Amoghasiddhi—and their retinues. These days cannot be measured in relative time; they last as long as our meditation allows them to last. A "day" merely refers to the recognition of and abiding in non-conceptual wisdom in relation to the appearance of a certain buddha. If we cannot abide in the first day, it will be over in an instant and the second day will begin.

The texts say that we will experience blinding lights streaming from the heart centers of the buddhas and their retinues to our heart centers. If we are mindful and aware that we are in the bardo state, we can recognize these lights as expressions of wisdom. Abiding in this state can lead us to liberation. Although we are free of body and mind, we still have habitual tendencies to see and hear as if we still inhabited a body. So if we have not mastered fearlessness, we will experience fear or aversion to the light shooting into the mind's "eyes"; at this time it is important not to have any impatience with this experience. The blinding lights are interspersed with pleasant calming lights; we must be careful not to generate attachment toward them.

Although ordinary practitioners acting as entrusted Dharma friends will not know exactly what we are experiencing after the outer breath has ceased, they should remind us that the appearances are arising from our own minds and not to generate attachment or aversion to the lights. This reminder should be given for at least a week after death.

Sometimes Western students wonder if, due to their different culture, they will see these buddhas differently than they appear in Tibetan thangkas, but their appearance depends more on habituation than culture. Only those with strong habituation to practice will actually perceive any of the Wisdom Buddhas; others with less practice or without training may see only light. All appearances arise based on your own grasping and attachment, and appear in a unique way according to your karma and your state of mind. It is more important to understand how appearances arise in the mind rather than the form they take. If we get too attached to the forms that arise, we will be distracted from the practice of meditation and our fundamental goals—to experience bodhichitta and abide in the view at the time of death. Any visual expression of form or color is not really important; rather, we must learn to liberate those expressions the moment they arise, so that we are without grasping.

The Peaceful and Wrathful Deities

After the five days of meditative concentration pass, the forty-two peaceful deities appear. Again, there will be blinding and pleasant lights toward which we must generate neither fear nor attachment. Due to our strong habitual tendencies, we may not recognize these appearances as expressions of our own mind and may lose the opportunities that go with the stage of the appearance of the peaceful deities.

On the seventh day, Vidyadharas, or "awareness holders," will appear along with wisdom dakinis, again accompanied by blinding and pleasant lights. If we are still without recognition, the fifty-eight wrathful deities will appear on the eighth day. Because these appearances are so terrifying, we can prepare ourselves to great benefit by looking at such images now until we no longer find them terrifying or distasteful. An authentic teacher can decide whether working with the wrathful deity practices is appropriate for our level.

Next, we will hear a loud, frightening sound like numerous thunderclaps. If we have not worked with sound as part of our daily practice, this experience can also lead to great fear and aversion. But if we are free of fear and recognize the noise as an expression of our own mind, then it can be a condition for liberation.

The next luminosity arises as lights that are almost blinding. The analogy given is that they are like weapons. These multi-colored lights are so bright it feels as if we are being stabbed with knives. Again, we must not generate fear or aversion.

The Four Types of Liberation

A Dzogchen yogi, who has taken up the lama's introduction to the nature of mind with extreme diligence, will recognize the sounds, lights, and rays as expressions of his or her own mind. This is the recognition of intrinsic wisdom, the wisdom of indivisible appearance and emptiness. Such a yogi would attain liberation into the Dharmakaya in the Bardo of Dying.

A great practitioner of "generation stage" yoga—the yoga in which one meditates on forms, sounds, and thoughts as having the nature of deities, mantras, and wisdom—will recognize the light and rays as the body of the yidam and retinue, and the sounds as mantra or sacred speech. With great habituation to meditation on the yidam deity, this type of practitioner will see all appearances as the yidam and attain the Sambhogakaya in the Bardo of Suchness.

A third type of yogi, who sees illusory appearances as empty, attains the Nirmanakaya liberation. Someone who has diligently trained and has strong habituation to seeing phenomena as illusory will not grasp at the sounds, lights, and rays as real, but will naturally perceive them as dreamlike and insubstantial.

A fourth type of liberation is possible for a yogi who realizes that all appearances in samsara and nirvana arise from the mind, or are "self-arisen." With this habituation, the yogi will recognize the appearances in the bardo as expressions of the mind and will achieve the liberation of Rupakaya, or the "essence body."

The texts say that we should examine these four types of meditation to see which one suits our aptitude or natural ability. Then we should train in that type of meditation with extreme diligence. This will enhance our ability to attain liberation through that particular method.

The Bardo of Existence

If we have not been able to recognize the experiences in the Bardo of Suchness as expressions of our own mind and attain liberation, we will enter the Bardo of Existence. For the majority of beings, this bardo state lasts about forty-nine days. After that we will take birth according to our karma and habitual tendencies. Yet, in the Bardo of Existence, it is still possible to influence where we will take birth.

The Bardo of Existence is a state where almost anything can appear. As in dreams, we may feel that we are falling down into a deep hole or that weapons are hitting us from behind. It is most beneficial if we have practiced recognizing our dreams in the Dream Bardo and can apply this to the Bardo of Existence. When we recognize that we are dreaming, we have the ability to take action. For example, if we are at the top of a cliff we can make a decision to jump rather than fall. We can transcend fear; this is very useful training.

If a lama were practicing for our benefit for forty-nine days, he or she would constantly be reminding us that all appearances before us are like dreams, that anything appearing in our mind is a manifestation of the three poisons. He or she would read to us the important instructions that we were given in our lifetime. If we are able to recognize that we are in the Bardo of Existence, we can pray with devotion to our yidam deity and ask to take rebirth in that deity's pure land. In that case we can transcend taking birth in the womb, taking birth instead in a realm that is beneficial for Dharma practice.

If we have been unable to use any of the opportunities up to this point, we still have one last chance to choose parents who will be supportive of Dharma practice. If we have mindfulness, our consciousness can choose to be born in a supportive family endowed with compassion. If we have had no training in mindfulness, then we will simply take birth according to our karma as one of the six types of sentient beings.

The idea of a *tulku,* or emanation of a bodhisattva, has become popular these days. If we have the ability to choose the realm in which to take birth, we would visualize the father and mother as Vajrasattva and his consort, Vajratopa. Upon entering the womb, we would visualize our own mind awareness as a blue HUNG syllable or the heart mantra of our yidam deity. It would then be possible to take birth as a tulku or as an emanation of a wisdom being. It would be helpful to have a picture or a thangka of Vajrasattva and Vajratopa to study and keep in our meditation room to help us recognize our parents as deities when we take birth.

We need a strong visualization practice or we will not be able to visualize Vajrasattva and his consort. We also need great mindfulness and compassion. In order to practice in the bardos we must increase our mindfulness each day and become accustomed to abiding in the view. We should receive instruction on the Dream Bardo and how to recognize that we are dreaming and to meditate in our dreams. We must develop faith and devotion. There are many stories of practitioners of guru yoga, the practice of mixing one's mind with the teacher's mind, who remembered their root teacher in the bardos and were liberated!

9

THE PRACTICE OF PHOWA

I RECEIVED THIS phowa teaching from my root lama, Kyabje Tsara Dharmakirti Rinpoche, who was a realized master of the Longchen Nyingthig lineage. The blessing is particularly profound when such a teaching is directly passed on from a pure lineage. The teaching I am giving here is very condensed, yet still has all that is necessary to understand how to use this practice for ourselves and others.

To fulfill the aspirations of our Dharma Visions and approach death with confidence, we must have both an intimate knowledge of the signs of death and mastery of the practice of phowa. Many students receive phowa teachings, but often they do not put the teachings into regular practice. Without practice, their once-strong faith in Dharma is slowly eroded. Various texts state that if, at the time of death, we have not made an adequate effort and mastered techniques of meditation or instructions from our lama, we could be filled with regret and fear. In this case, our death would be accompanied by strong afflictions and turn out to have even worse consequences than that of an untrained person. If an entrusted Dharma friend or a lama comes to help us in this situation, how will they be able to guide us?

Mastery of phowa can be potent enough to be useful even if we have not mastered other techniques. Phowa is a method that we can rely upon in the Bardo of Dying. It is important for Dharma practitioners to make the effort to learn phowa and practice it periodically so they can actually use it at the time of death.

There are five types of phowa that I will talk about briefly here to help us understand the possibilities for liberation that can result from sincere practice.

The Dharmakaya Phowa

When we abide in the Dharmakaya at the time of death, we practice the supreme type of phowa and attain "liberation without entering the bardo state." As we mentioned earlier, this is for a practitioner of the most excellent capacity and is attained by very few. Mastery is based on supreme diligence as well as being completely free of any doubts about the view. Such a practitioner is not only able to abide in the view during practice but in the post-meditation state as well.

Dharmakaya phowa depends on a lama introducing us to the nature of mind. The lama reminds us that all beings have buddha-nature, the cause for realization. Based on this introduction, it may be possible to abide in intrinsic wisdom as the outer breath ceases. Our life-long training would culminate in recognizing the ground luminosity as indivisible from the nature of mind to which we have been introduced by our lama.

In order to accomplish this, we must have a long-term, unwavering commitment to practice, great faith, good karma, and an uncommonly close relationship with a lama. We must have cut through any doubts about the view. Knowing this should motivate us to practice and to be diligent in our training, especially in using analysis and contemplation together to cut through any doubts. I want to emphasize again the importance of relying upon an authentic teacher who has mastered these teachings. Then it is possible for us to apply for our "phowa visa" and be able to use it!

The Sambhogakaya Phowa

Practitioners of middle capacity practice Sambhogakaya phowa. This is the union of the generation and perfection stages, two stages of practice in the Secret Mantrayana teachings. When we say that these two are indivisible, we are talking about purifying all appearances and seeing them as the deity and, at the same time, recognizing the empty nature of appearances and abiding in the union of these two. At the time of death, when appearances arise in the mind, practitioners of this phowa recognize all of these appearances as the mandala, a celestial palace, or the yidam deity. Based on that recognition, liberation is attained.

We must train diligently through contemplation and through abiding in the view to cultivate the conviction that all things are illusory. This will cut through our grasping to appearances as being real. Then, whatever appearances are in front of us will not matter at all. We will simply think to ourselves, "This is illusory, like a dream; this is an expression of my own mind." Then appearances will lose their power over us.

The Nirmanakaya Phowa

The third type of phowa is Nirmanakaya phowa. This type of phowa is actually the pathway for the birth of a *tulku*, or reincarnated lama. It is based on an immeasurable motivation of compassion for sentient beings. A master of meditation who wishes to take birth in a certain realm would obtain the ripening empowerments from his or her lama, receive bodhisattva and Vajrayana vows, and become extremely skillful at the generation and perfection stages. After death, the consciousness of the practitioner would go through the bardo states until the Bardo of Existence and take birth as a tulku, a realized being who is able to benefit others.

Transference Based on Three Metaphors

The fourth type of phowa is called *transference based on three metaphors*. This enables us to practice the transference of our own consciousness. It is appropriate for anyone at any point on the path. Milarepa said that phowa is a path that can be practiced by those who lack experience or who are not highly skilled at meditation. This is very appropriate for Western students who may not yet have developed a great capacity to practice meditation. It is also said that for a being who has cultivated non-virtue, phowa can fiercely purify that karma. So even for that being, phowa is an accessible practice. However, we should not think of this type of phowa as only being for beginning practitioners. This is a practice that each and every student of the Vajrayana should master during their lifetime.

THE THREE METAPHORS TO RELY UPON

Traditionally, three metaphors are relied upon to illustrate the effectiveness of this type of phowa practice, and how it is possible to send the consciousness out of this physical body. Here is brief description and exploration of each of them:

> ► The first metaphor depicts the central channel as the path. In order to go to a particular destination, we need a path, a way to get there. So, in phowa practice, the path is the central channel going straight up the body from the navel area to the top of the head.

▸ The second metaphor depicts the consciousness as a traveler. The meaning of this metaphor is that our consciousness isn't always going to be in the same body or in the same place. It moves around. In this case, it is going to move out of the present body.

▸ The third metaphor depicts the pure land, the "dwelling place" of enlightened beings, as the consciousness' destination. We visualize it about an arrow's length above our heads.

When we practice phowa based on the three metaphors, from the point of view of conventional reality, our ordinary way of thinking, we are sending the consciousness to a pure land, seen as our home or birthplace. From the point of view of ultimate reality, we are simply sending the consciousness into the unborn Dharmakaya. We can rely on either of these two views depending on our level of experience.

The great protector Maitreya said that when one realizes the state of equality, or the nature of mind, there are no lower realms or lower births. All is the expression of a pure land. We often think of the pure realms of realized beings as existing somewhere outside of us. It is important to realize that, in regards to a pure land, there is no place to go. The only pure realm is mastery of the mind.

Our own perception is dominated by impurity. We don't need many reminders of how agitated our minds become by outer conditions; we are constantly upset by situations that we view impurely. Perhaps while we are walking we are approached by someone who is begging or someone that we don't like, and we become disturbed and agitated. This has to do with our inner experience and the way that we perceive the world. Yet it is possible to purify the mind so that we see all as a pure land.

When we speak about a bodhisattva being realized, it means that he or she can see beyond duality, beyond attachment or dislike. A bodhisattva cannot be harmed by outer things. This is all the result of mastery over the mind. We can calmly bear the outer things that tend to hurt us; we have the ability to transform our suffering.

During the stages of appearance, increase, attainment, and full attainment, there are many opportunities for us to practice phowa for ourselves. When the white essence, or *thigle,* of the father moves from the head toward the heart, we "see" a vast sky permeated with the light of the moon. Here is our first opportunity to practice after the outer breath has ceased. This begins the three-fold stage during which the three poisons naturally cease. Anger dissolves during the stage of appearance, desire during the stage of increase, and ignorance during the stage of attainment. Examining this logically, it makes sense that the process of dying is described as the easiest time to attain liberation. In our normal experience, we are constantly afflicted by the three poisons, but here there is a very short period of time when the three poisons naturally cease.

We must learn to recognize when to start our phowa practice. During the time that the five sense faculties are dissolving, our awareness is very clear. This is the time when it is easiest to practice phowa for ourselves. If we don't recognize that we are dying until the later stages, it becomes more difficult.

Phowa for Others

Some practitioners may aspire not only to remind the dying person of their phowa practice and read the text to them, but also to practice a type of phowa for someone who is in the process of dying or who has died. Based on our own mastery of phowa, it is possible to practice for another being.

When we take up the practice of phowa for others, we need to work with a technique of visualization that is characterized by unmovable, undistracted concentration. Additionally, we should cultivate superior bodhichitta for beings everywhere who are suffering.

If we wish to do phowa for others, the most important thing is to recognize when the person is actually dying. It could be harmful to practice at the wrong time. The proper time to do phowa for another is when the outer breath has ceased and the inner breath is still viable. Even if you do not have an unmistaken experience of the view, it is possible to benefit a person simply by virtue of the state of mind of the dying person at that time.

To learn how to practice phowa for others, we must receive instructions from our lama or an authentic teacher who has practiced phowa extensively, mastered it, and experienced signs of accomplishment. Also, I encourage students to attend several phowa retreats, accumulate at least three weeks of intensive practice, attain the signs of phowa, and continue with regularly spaced practice sessions. Of course, it is impossible to help others without having compassion and bodhichitta; with strong bodhichitta we may still be able to help another even if the signs of phowa have not appeared. You do not have to be a highly realized practitioner to do phowa for another person if you do it at the right time and do the practice properly. It would be especially beneficial to have several people doing the phowa practice together.

The signs of accomplishing phowa are generally described as: an opening on the top of the head where the head touches the central channel or a bump on the head in the same place; being able to stick a blade of grass in the wound, which oozes light-colored fluid; nausea, headache, and sweating.

Once the inner breath has ceased, it is very difficult to benefit the person through phowa practice. The great master Padmasambhava said that if we are not completely realized, helping a person after the inner breath has ceased is most difficult; only a great master may be able to help at this time. The traditional analogy is that the consciousness is like a bewildered dog wandering from place to place. It is greatly upset and therefore harder to help. An untrained individual will not be certain they have died and will become very confused. The mind in this state moves quickly from place to place and is aware of many things at once.

Practices for Someone Who Has Died Suddenly

If an experienced chod practitioner is available, they should be invited to do chod and phowa for the deceased. This is especially beneficial if that person was young and healthy and died in an accident. A lama with strong bodhichitta can also be invited to do a wrathful practice like Vajrakilaya during or even after the forty-nine days following death. A practice like this can be requested through contacting a Buddhist monastery or an organization like the Phowa Foundation.

If the person has committed suicide, chod or wrathful practices are done by accomplished practitioners. If a practitioner is not experienced at practicing chod, it is better to do the Heart Sutra practice or the Dorje Chodpa practice. Any bodhichitta practice will benefit the person, along with dedicating meritorious acts. In Tibet, the body of someone who has committed suicide is usually buried or offered to birds. Any sudden death is a result of obstacles, so chod practice is done rather than burning the body.

10

INSTRUCTIONS FOR THE PRACTICE OF PHOWA

—⁂—

IN THIS SECTION, I will give instructions on *Phowa: Buddhahood without Meditation*, a text from the Longchen Nyingthig tradition. If you have received instructions from your own lama using a different text, you should practice with that text. The basic instructions are the same, even if there are slight variations in the visualizations used. If you have never received phowa instruction, you may practice this visualization, but you should request the transmission and further teachings from an authentic teacher when possible.

Preparation for the Practice

You might begin your practice session by doing yoga postures, tai chi, or stretching, as the movement of the body helps the mind to relax and makes it easier to abide. Notice the relationship between the body and what arises in the mind. You can do all kinds of movement; you can sing or dance. Then when you sit down to practice, notice what kind of energy arises in the mind. In my opinion, it is good to experiment with conditions for practice. It can be very difficult to relax when you do not move before sitting down. Now, as you prepare yourself to practice, be very careful to sit with your spine as straight as an arrow in order that the central channel that runs through the body from your navel to the top of your head will also be completely straight. As I said earlier, the central channel is the path for your consciousness to leave the body. When the central channel is straight, then the wind energy within the body moves more easily; this enables you to abide in the essence of mind or to recognize wisdom more easily. You can experiment with your posture: examine what your mind is like when you sit straight and then when you slouch over. You will experience a difference.

Take some time to reflect on the foundational ideas of Buddhism such as impermanence and compassion, and generate bodhichitta before you begin your practice. Try to abide in the recognition that the entire environment around you is empty of inherent existence. From the expression of emptiness, visualize everything around you as a completely pure realm or celestial palace.

In my lineage, we always begin phowa practice with the *Meditation on the Great Compassionate One*, a practice of Avalokiteshvara, in order to generate compassion and bodhichitta for all beings. I recommend using this (see Appendix I) or a similar sadhana to begin your practice.

Many of the practices I describe involve some elements of visualization. Since some students find visualization difficult at first, here are some points that may help you.

▸ Visualize with your eyes open or halfway open. If you are not used to doing this, you can alternate visualizing with open and closed eyes and work up to keeping the eyes open.

▸ Visualization is a skill that is developed slowly. The more mind stability you have, the more precise your visualization. Actually, visualization trains you in the skills of shamatha. Go slowly and build your skill over time.

▶ Visualization is devotional, but if you make too much effort, it becomes dogmatic and difficult. In the beginning, visualization is about relating to the energy of the deity as being present or just holding the aspiration that the deity is present.

▶ Begin by looking at a picture of the deity associated with your visualization. Then visualize the picture in your mind. When it is no longer clear, go back and look at the picture. Move back and forth between the picture and the visualization. Slowly, your ability to hold the image longer will increase. You can also do this by visualizing just the head first, then adding the torso, the legs, and so forth.

▶ Look at the picture and, without blinking, scan from the top of the head to the bottom. Then visualize the image in your mind. Again, go back and forth in this way until there is some stability in your visualization.

The Practice

In the center of this pure realm or celestial palace, visualize yourself as Vajrayogini. This is one form of Yeshe Tsogyal, the consort of Padmasambhava. Her countenance is both peaceful and wrathful. She is red in color and has one face and two arms. In her right hand she is holding a skulldrum and in her left hand a hooked knife, symbolizing the cutting through of attachment and ignorance as well as the impermanence of life.

If you are skilled in visualization, you can visualize garlands of skulls and precious stones around her neck. She is in dancing posture, standing on her left leg with her right knee raised and her foot touching the left thigh. She is standing on rotting corpses, which are resting upon carpets of a lotus and the sun. These corpses symbolize the cutting through of fear, impurity, and the ego.

Visualize yourself as Vajrayogini with the central channel going straight up your body. The central channel opens at the top of the head so the consciousness can move out. About three fingers below the navel, the central channel is closed by a knot.

The thickness of the central channel is that of the shaft of an arrow. It is hollow so that the consciousness can move through it. It is a clean, pure, hollow, empty channel.

There are four characteristics of the central channel. You can visualize them or just think about them.

- ▸ The first characteristic is that the central channel is a bright indigo blue color, the symbol of the unchanging Dharmakaya.

- ▸ The second is that the actual fabric of the central channel is fine like lotus petals. The symbolic meaning is that the veils of the obscurations of habitual tendencies that cover the mind are as fine as lotus petals.

- ▸ The third is that the central channel is bright as if illuminated by a lamp, symbolizing the dispelling of the darkness of ignorance.

► The fourth is that the central channel is completely straight, which symbolizes that this practice will not lead one to the lower realms but to the higher realms.

You should not have a fixed idea of where the central channel touches the top of the head, as it can vary from person to person.

If visualization is difficult, you can simply reflect on the qualities of the central channel. Reflection will give you useful support. Greater detail about the central channel can be found in Patrul Rinpoche's *Words of my Perfect Teacher.*

Inside the heart center, at the base of the heart, visualize a sphere of green light energy (the wind energy) the size of a pea. On top of it is a red HRI syllable, vibrant and quivering. The HRI is your own mind or consciousness, and the heart is its natural resting place.

Now the self-visualization is complete and we turn to the space above, where you are sending your consciousness. If your death is quickly approaching, you might be lying down. You should try to sit up if you can, but if you can't, don't worry; this is essentially a devotional practice and so you shouldn't worry exactly where you visualize.

About an arrow's length above the opening at the top of the head, visualize a precious throne. Seated upon a lotus with cushions of the sun and the moon is the essence of your root lama, but with the appearance of Buddha Amitabha, red and adorned with luminous light. If you are not used to visualizing, you can simply think with devotion that all of this is present and is the essence of your lama. You can also look at a thangka to help you.

Again, the complexity of the visualization above you depends on your own practice. The best possible visualization is the whole retinue of Buddha Amitabha's bodhisattvas. Alternately, you can visualize Avalokiteshvara standing to the right of Amitabha, white in color with one face and four arms, and to the left is blue Vajrapani with one face and two arms, wrathful and also standing.

After visualizing yourself as Vajrayogini with Amitabha in the sky above, you begin the actual practice of phowa. The important thing is not to recite the words of the practice just by rote, but to generate faith and actually work on cultivating whatever is being said in the text. In this text is the recitation of buddhas' names. You are calling to each named buddha to invoke their compassionate energy.

> Recite the syllable HRI five times, and visualize that the energy of the recitation is pushing the glowing green sphere that symbolizes your wind energy and the HRI that symbolizes your consciousness together upward through the central channel. As you say the fifth HRI, visualize your consciousness at the top of your head. At that point, recite the syllables HI-KA either seven or twenty-one times as you visualize the essence of your mind shooting up into the heart center of Buddha Amitabha. With each repetition the green sphere goes up to his heart center and comes back down to the opening at the top of your central channel. After the last HI-KA, the consciousness comes all the way back down to your heart center and again rests on the joint in the central channel.

The syllables may be recited differently by practitioners of different lineages. The Longchen Nyingthig lineage does not vocalize the KA. In some lineages they say the syllable HI (pronounced HEE) to send the consciousness up, and the KA as it comes back down. Some-times the HI-KA is done seven times or sometimes twenty-one times. Great practitioners may only do it three or five times. This depends on your ability to abide in the nature of mind. If you are able to abide for a period of time, then it is not necessary to send the conscious-ness up so many times.

Additionally, more experienced practitioners should bring the green sphere all the way back down into the heart center with each recitation of HI-KA. Less experienced practitioners can send the green sphere up once, and then bring it back down to the top of the central channel, and then send it up and down from there for the remaining recitations. On the last HI-KA, the green sphere can then drop back down into the heart center.

There are many opportunities in one recitation of the phowa text to practice sending the consciousness up. It is good to keep visual-izing the consciousness being sent up the central channel or at least thinking that this is what is happening.

When the great master Milarepa was quite young and had very little experience, he went to practice phowa for someone who had died. He didn't know all the instructions well, and so visualized the person's body like a cistern of water and their consciousness as a big ball of yarn. Despite his non-traditional practice, his devotion was so great that he liberated the person's consciousness. That should tell you that even if you can't visualize perfectly but you have great devotion, aspiration, and bodhichitta, then this practice will still be beneficial.

At the end of your phowa practice, the Amitabha that you have visualized transforms into Amitayus, the Long-Life Buddha. Amitayus is the Sambhogakaya form of Buddha Amitabha. Amitayus dissolves into you, and you visualize yourself as Amitayus as you say the long-life mantra: OM A MA RA NI DZI WEN TI YE SO HA. You should repeat the mantra at least one hundred times or, if possible, two to three hundred times. This is to seal the practice and create dependent arising for practicing at the time of death, so be sure to do this carefully. *This is very important; do not ever skip this when you are practicing on your own.* It is also said that reciting the long-life mantra following phowa practice can actually create the conditions for a long life.

If you are at the moment of death and cannot practice phowa, which is a definite possibility, simply turn your eyes upward and focus on the top of your head. If a lama or entrusted Dharma friend is practicing phowa for you, this will make it much easier for them. At the time of death, your consciousness will be very heavy, so even the simple effort of turning your eyes upward will make it lighter and easier for someone to help lift it out of you. If you are acting as an entrusted Dharma friend, remind the dying person to turn his or her eyes upward at this time. You can help by touching the top of the head or pulling gently on the hair there.

When you are training in phowa, you should take a break when any of the signs of accomplishment appear. Then either practice in very short sessions or perhaps only once a month. You don't want to continue and make yourself feel ill.

If you were to be in a situation like a car accident where you knew you were going to die immediately, simply turning your gaze upward and bringing your attention to the top of the head will be helpful. Bringing the awareness to the top of the head is something you can practice in your daily life. Someone who understands how to abide in the nature of mind will find that turning the eyes upward naturally helps with that, so it is a good thing to do in any situation.

At the end of the phowa text is a section called the "Phowa of Ultimate Reality." It uses the syllable PHET, and a practitioner who knows how to abide in the nature of mind should do so after repeating the syllable.

11

When Death Is Near

———⚬———

When we become aware of signs that death is near, we should make an extra effort at practicing phowa. We should read the instructions for phowa over and over and practice the text at least once a day if possible. We should also be practicing our yidam practice daily. When not formally practicing, we can repeat the names of the buddhas given in the phowa text. It is also good to take or re-take bodhisattva vows whenever the opportunity arises. If we know we are going to die but our senses have not yet started to dissolve, we should invite our entrusted Dharma friends to take the bodhisattva and bodhichitta vows together with us if it is at all possible. We should also start (or intensify our practice of) making offerings for the benefit of others. If we are unable to make material offerings, then they should at least be made mentally, offering them perfectly and without attachment from our minds.

Buddhist texts state that, when death is imminent, we should make threefold offerings to help lengthen our lives, such as saving the lives of animals or insects who are going to die or be killed. It is important, however, that we do not take this as license to dwell on the timing of our impending death or become attached to the idea of lengthening our lives. These offerings can indeed create favorable conditions based on the inconceivable expression of dependent arising.

Rather than becoming sad, we can use the possibility of death to motivate ourselves to continue to practice and accumulate virtue. We can make offerings to the buddhas and bodhisattvas, as well as our supreme spiritual friend, ordinary beings, and the sangha to support their practice. It is best for us to approach death without attachments. In Tibet, it is said that great practitioners die with only the clothes on their backs and their meditation cushions.

Preparing the Environment

There are a number of external preparations we can make for death. An altar should be set up so we can easily see it from our bed. A small table or dresser top can be used for statues, photos of our yidam deity, lama, or any spiritual guide we feel a connection with, and any other ritual items. Friends can hang thangkas on the walls, arrange flowers, and light candles if permitted. The room should be set up beautifully! As we discussed earlier, all of the items we wish to be on the altar should already be in our Dharma Box or we should have previously arranged with our entrusted Dharma friends or family members to bring specific items from our home altar.

It is best to be in a quiet place when we are dying; if one is a very experienced practitioner, it is also beneficial to be alone, but most of us will need guides and helpers. If we do not have great stability in meditation, we can easily become distracted at this time. Being around loved ones can generate significant attachment and their crying could become an obstacle to practice. The entrusted Dharma friend can remind us to stay calm, to remember our practice, and to be patient with others.

There are many other aids to liberation that can help a dying person. One of these is liberation through tasting, or *nyungdrol*. *Dutsi*, or ritually prepared blessed pills, can be kept in our Dharma Box. One pill can be put in a small bottle of water each day, or a few bottles can be prepared and kept in the refrigerator. If we are well enough to do so ourselves, we can sip on this anytime we wish, both before the signs of death appear and throughout their appearance. If we are very weak, our entrusted Dharma friends can help us to do so. We should be sure to have this written into our Dharma Will as we may not remember or be able to prepare it ourselves.

Other aids are liberation through hearing the Dharma (*tudrol*); liberation by wearing (*dagdrol*), which is done by wearing a special mandala on the body (see chapter 13); liberation through touch (*raktrol*), which occurs through a realized being's touch; and liberation through sight (*tongdrol*), which would occur based on seeing a thangka of the One Hundred Peaceful and Wrathful Deities, Samantabhadra (Kuntuzangpo), or a yidam deity.

If possible, we should be mindful of our posture at the time of death. Buddha Shakyamuni died while resting in the "lion's pose," a posture for maintaining awareness even as we sleep or die. Each part of the posture supports a part of the mind, allowing it to remain clear. It allows for the proper placement of the channels so that energy may flow easily, and actually facilitates the non-arising of anger, fear, or attachment as we are dying. The posture not only creates good dependent arising and the conditions to die mindfully, but also emulates the realization of Buddha Shakyamuni. Ideally, we should lie on our right side with our head to the north and our chin slightly lowered toward the chest, head resting on the right palm. The left arm should rest on the left thigh. If we are not able to do this, we should at least try to have our head toward the north. We can practice this each night as we fall asleep so that we can become habituated to lying in this position.

The last and most important preparation we can make, as we feel death approaching, is to try to cut through all desire and attachment to this life and this body so we can rest in the nature of mind itself. Once the attachments and afflictive emotions are cut through, we should generate bodhichitta and pray that for all future lives, we will be able to benefit sentient beings.

Preparing the Mind

Tonglen (literally, "sending and taking") is a valuable practice to engage in throughout your life, and especially as you learn that death is approaching.

First, we should reflect on the fact that all beings in samsara must go through the experience of death. We can think that there are innumerable beings in the world who are about to die at this same exact moment. Because we are all human beings, we are all experiencing the same kinds of emotions. We could begin with the aspiration:

> *For all those beings who are facing death like I am, may they be liberated from fear and endowed with happiness.*

This is an example of training in the self as equal to others. When you feel confident and able to make this wish sincerely for others, then train in exchanging yourself for others:

> *For all those beings who are facing death at the same time as I am, may I take on all of their fear and suffering; may I take on any of their non-virtue or anything that causes them mental distress, and may they all be endowed with happiness and peace.*

Train in that aspiration for some time, because it is a big aspiration and can be frightening. Finally, you can work at making others more important than yourself, thinking:

> *May my root of virtue of the three times ripen in all beings who are suffering, and may all of their non-virtue without exception ripen in me.*

This is the most vast and powerful aspiration that we can generate through the practice of tonglen.

The most important thing we can do at the time of death is to have the motivation of bodhichitta and a virtuous thought in mind. It would be beneficial to have a prayer that we have already trained in to help us achieve this goal.

We can use the brief prayer below or we can write something in our own words.

> *In this lifetime I have had the opportunity to receive and practice the teachings of Dharma. I have received bodhisattva vows and Secret Mantrayana vows. If I have broken or contradicted these vows in any way, at this moment I regret this from my heart and apologize. From this day forward and in all of my future lives, may I be born into a perfectly pure precious human life endowed with the ability to practice the Dharma. Until I attain complete buddhahood, may I serve as Avalokiteshvara and Vajrapani served to benefit all beings.*

The aspiration prayer that we compose as part of our Dharma Vision can also be used in this way and read each night before we go to sleep. Then we will remember it easily at the time of death.

Our entrusted Dharma friends can read it to us and remind us of our aspirations. We should place a copy of this in the binder of prayers in our Dharma Box. Having a specific prayer like this at the time of death can influence our rebirth positively.

Each night before we go to sleep, we can think, "I am about to go to sleep and I may not wake up tomorrow. This may be the last time I have a conscious thought." If we can train in having a virtuous thought in mind every night as we go to sleep, that will become a good condition to have that same thought at the time of death.

The scriptures say that even if we have accumulated a lot of non-virtue during our lifetime, having this kind of pristine motivation at the time of death as our last thought will cause us to attain a precious human life for at least a few lifetimes. If we attain that, we will have a further chance to purify our minds and our karma. This last thought could influence all our lifetimes to come, so it is most important to train in this and to be without anger and attachment at the moment of death.

When we are sick, we can be more impatient than usual. As we come closer to the moment of death, we can become very agitated. In this case, it is important for those around us to be very mindful and to only say things that are supportive and calming. The entrusted Dharma friends should try to help family and friends abandon their self-attachment and thoughts of losing a loved one; they should be helped to focus on offering strength and encouragement, rather than having outbursts, weeping in their loved one's presence, or doing anything that would make it difficult to cut through self-attachment. Prayers and mantras help the mind to be quiet.

If our friends and family focus on a simple prayer or aspiration at that time, it will offer solace and strength simply by surrounding us with loving energy.

———— ⸻ᴡ⸻ ————

When It Is Time to Die

Take Refuge and Bodhichitta Vows

Even if we have already taken these vows, we should take them again. An entrusted Dharma friend can remind us by reading them out loud. If we have a yidam practice, these vows will already be included in the text. Otherwise, a copy of the vows should be in our Dharma Box for this purpose.

Read our Practices and Texts

Our entrusted Dharma friends can then read any daily reading or oral instructions from our root lama (see special instructions for this in chapter 15), our yidam and phowa practices, and whatever lineage practices for the dead we have requested (*The Tibetan Book of the Dead*, for example, is from the Nyingma lineage but can be used for anyone if they so desire). We can also listen to recordings of phowa practice and *The Tibetan Book of the Dead*, as well as recordings of mantras.

When our entrusted Dharma friends read the phowa text aloud, they can first read the visualization given in this book and then the actual practice, reminding us of the instructions to send our consciousness out with the syllable *HRI*. Or if a lama is present, he or she will practice phowa for us before the outer breath ceases.

Focus on the Top of the Head

We spoke earlier about getting used to placing our awareness at the top of the head. We should be reminded to do so now. If we are not experienced practitioners, an entrusted Dharma friend can place his or her fingers on the top of our head or gently pull the hair there while saying one of the prayers we have requested. The Prayer of Kuntuzangpo, or other dedication prayers, would be appropriate at this time.

KNOW THAT ALL APPEARANCES ARISE FROM THE MIND

All the great masters have said that the best thing one can do for a dying person is to tell them that all appearances arise from the mind. The entrusted Dharma friend can whisper in our ear, "You are going to die soon. Know that all appearances—even if they are terrifying—are arising from your own mind." They should repeat this many times.

If we are not conscious to receive verbal instructions, entrusted Dharma friends can recite the names of two buddhas in particular. These are Buddha Ratnaketu and the Medicine Buddha (Sangye Menla). Both made aspirations that anyone hearing their names would be benefitted by them. The entrusted Dharma friend should also continue to read our practices to us.

12

How to Help Someone through the Dying Process

—◊◊◊◊—

Practicing Tonglen for Someone Who Is Dying

As a beginning practitioner, it is very hard to think of taking on another person's pain and suffering. Even though we care about that person very much, it can still be frightening when we see someone in pain at the time of death. It can also be frightening to think about taking on that suffering due to our own self-attachment.

In order to actually practice tonglen, where we generate the aspiration to take on another person's pain and suffering, we need to reflect on the fact that all people have to die. It is just a matter of when. From that point of view, self and others are equal. Just like when we discussed practicing tonglen at the time of our own death, we can start by contemplating the equality of self and other; after we feel confident of this equality, we can try to actually exchange our happiness for another's suffering.

At first we can think that we are taking on the negative karma of the dying person. We recognize that the person before us is facing death and that they are experiencing much pain and suffering. They have regrets and think they have made many mistakes in their lives.

This causes them mental torment. They are also afraid to carry those mistakes with them when they die; they are afraid of what will happen to them after they die as a result of their mistaken actions. We have that in common with them; it is human for us to regret the things we have done wrong during our lives. We, too, would not want to take the suffering or negativity that we have accumulated with us at the time of death. We can reflect on how much peace and joy we would feel at death if there was a person willing to take on our pain and suffering, and the negativity we had accumulated throughout our lifetime.

There are many visualization practices for tonglen, such as seeing the other person's suffering or non-virtue as a black cloud and bringing that energy into yourself. We can practice this by working with the breath: when we exhale, we think we are sending out our happiness and virtue to the person who is dying, that it is simply radiating out of us; when we breathe in, we think about their suffering coming into us. For some people, this may be difficult to do. In that case, we can instead focus on any compassion practice.

A hospice worker told me recently about something she sees quite often: family members don't want to see the dying person as they come closer to death, or to witness his or her death. The dying person is left alone, even though the family may have been close before this. We should really reflect on the equality of self and other, and think about how we would feel if people close to us didn't want to see us when we were dying, in order to avoid their own suffering. Instead we should do what we can to comfort and support the dying person.

We may not be able to practice tonglen or truly feel we can take on the dying person's suffering, but we can still reflect on how we are also going to have to die and we can feel great compassion toward him or her.

The Three Days Following Death

When the outer breath ceases, we should continue to read *The Tibetan Book of the Dead* or the text of another lineage to the person who has died. We should remind our friend of the signs that will now appear and to not be attached to them, saying, "All appearances are arising from your own mind." We should also continue to do phowa and read any oral instructions on the nature of mind that our friend has received, if we are qualified to read them. We can recite mantras as well. The Kuntuzangpo Prayer or a similar prayer can be used as a dedication when prayers are completed.

Our friend's Dharma Will should include any instructions on how they wish to have his or her body handled after death. We should do our best to follow these instructions, but it is important to recognize that all of their wishes may not be possible. We should do what we can, but it is more important that everyone's prayers and efforts are done with the motivation of bodhichitta.

Buddhist texts instruct us to leave a person's body unmoved for three days after the outer breath ceases. It may be difficult in Western society for this to happen. If a practitioner is dying in a hospital or at home, once the signs of death appear all of the above practices can be done so that they are complete before the body is taken anywhere. If there is very little time for some reason, then at least the refuge and bodhisattva vows, daily practice, and phowa should be done. If the person was a good practitioner, they will recognize these practices and be able to use them. When these practices are complete, the body can be washed and moved.

If our friend is at home, or the hospital is willing to let family and friends have time with the deceased, then the following can be done for up to three days. That is when the inner breath is considered to have ceased.

If a lama is present, he or she will perform *pujas*, rituals, such as bardo practices, Avalokiteshvara or Amitabha practices, though a lama is able to do this whether or not he or she is with the body. If a lama is not present, friends should recite the mantra of Avalokiteshvara (OM MA NI PAD ME HUNG HRI), the Vajrasattva hundred-syllable mantra, and Amitabha Buddha's mantra (OM A MI TA BHA HRI).

If the body needs to be moved to a funeral home, it would be beneficial if permission were granted to light candles in the room where the body is placed. One candle should be placed on an altar if possible.

After the third day, a burial or cremation should follow. In Tibet, a puja is generally done at the site where the body is burned. Here, family and friends can gather and do some practices at the cemetery or at the cremation if they are allowed. The liberation-by-wearing mandala can be placed on the body, to be buried or burned with it, along with anything else specified in the Dharma Will. Friends and family can read prayers and recite mantras. The short Vajrasattva mantra, OM BENZA SATTO HUNG, can be recited. Of course, if a lama is present, he or she will offer appropriate prayers. If families are not allowed to be at the cremation, they may say the prayers at home during the time that the body is being burned.

If the body is not cremated, it is still possible for a lama to perform a fire offering if a lock of hair and nail clippings are sent to a monastery, and arrangements for that ceremony have been made. This acts as a purification for the deceased, by "burning" the non-virtuous actions and karma.

After the burial or cremation, families can do something virtuous for their loved one. It is meritorious to make charitable contributions in their loved one's name. The family can also decide to observe the vow of not killing and become vegetarian for a week or for the forty-nine days that Buddhist texts say it may take to traverse the bardo states. If they have a gathering of friends, they could serve vegetarian food. Practitioners who have organizations they would like their families to donate to or who would like their families to offer only vegetarian food at gatherings should add this to their Dharma Wills.

Over the next forty-nine days, the counting of which begins three days after the outer breath has ceased, it is helpful to continue to practice on the deceased's behalf. Family and friends of the deceased should light candles on the altar and pray. The person's picture can be placed on the altar if the family wishes, but it should not be placed up high. If someone is able to do phowa, they can take the picture and place it in front of them while they do it. Serious practitioners may want to continue reading *The Tibetan Book of the Dead*, do Vajrasattva and Avalokiteshvara practices, read Amitabha's Aspiration Prayer, keep to ritual fasting (*nyungne*) or do any yidam practice they have a strong connection with. Even if Dharma friends and family cannot practice for a long time each day, they should do something; for instance, reciting the buddhas' names, as in the Medicine Buddha practice, is easy for people to do.

Family and friends can make requests for lamas to perform phowa and chod and to make daily offerings for their loved one during this time. Acts of charity, releasing animals, observing the vow of no harm—all of these will benefit the loved one.

After the forty-nine days are over, the person's altar can be taken down and the ritual items dispersed—either to family and friends of the deceased or to a Dharma center. In Tibet, after one year has passed, we spend three days making special offerings and inviting lamas to pray for the deceased. It would be okay for the family and friends of the deceased to do the same here for one day.

Helping a Dying Person Who Is Not Buddhist

People are very open at the time of death. Talk to them about loving-kindness and bodhichitta. Remind them to let go of any anger, sadness, or fear, to accept what is happening, and to stay calm. Ask them to focus on the top of their head and to visualize any spiritual teacher or great being of wisdom with whom they feel a connection. Help them to have pure motivation at the moment of death by directing their thoughts toward good wishes, prayers for future lives, and what kind of person they wish to be in the next life. If they do not believe in future lives, then they can simply send love and compassion out to others. That will be of great benefit to them. We can also remind them that everyone is going to die; they are not alone in facing death.

13

LIBERATION BY WEARING

——⟋⟍——

IN THIS CHAPTER, I will give a brief teaching on attaining liberation based upon wearing a special mandala. Along with the mindfulness engendered by wearing this mandala while alive, immense blessings emanate from the numerous sacred mantras inscribed on it, both during our lives and at death.

The *Liberation-by-Wearing Tantra* is devoted to teachings on the mandala worn by practitioners for protection in life as well as death. It describes how the mandala is drawn; the blessing of wearing the mandala; the empowerment given by a lama for wearing it; what to practice after one has obtained the empowerment; how to wear the mandala while alive and how to place it on the body at the time of death; and how to read and recite the mantras. These instructions are for both the person preparing to die and those assisting the dying person. The tantra also tells us how the mandala should be burned when cremating the body and about the benefit and good qualities of doing this.

When a person of supreme mental faculty analyzes the mind's nature and both understands and abides in the knowing that there is nothing inherently established in the outer, inner, or secret aspects of the mind, that which arises is self-liberated. This is the supreme introduction given in the teachings on *Liberation-by-Wearing* and is from the ultimate point of view.

For those who are not of supreme faculty, what does "liberation by wearing" really mean? An explanation given in the *Dra Talgyur Root Tantra,* one of the seventeen Dzogchen tantras, says, "The essence of all is condensed within." This refers to the way the mantric syllables are arranged, and it lists all the numerous mantras and mantric syllables found on this mandala. Among these are the essential mantras of all the Secret Mantrayana tantras: the essential mantras of body, speech, and mind; the essential mantra of Samantabhadra and Samantabhadri indivisible; the heart mantras of the five wisdoms; the Sambhogakaya mantras; and the mantra of the hundred peaceful and wrathful deities. They are all arranged on the mandala; thus, "the essence of all is condensed within."

We say liberation is possible due to the arrangement of all these very powerful sacred syllables and mantras. Simply wearing this mandala or having it placed on the body creates the condition for an incredibly strong blessing to occur; for this reason we say it can be a cause for liberation.

The omniscient master Longchenpa said that, by this mandala simply touching the body, our virtue will increase and our non-virtue will be purified more easily. It benefits us by keeping obstacles from arising and keeps us from getting ill. It helps improve our meditation. Even the place in which we abide is said to receive a special blessing— as though it is located near a stupa. If the mandala is placed on the heart center of a yogi who has trained in meditation during his or her lifetime, it enables the yogi to recognize the stages of dissolution and aspects of the bardo.

For beings of lesser faculty—those who have accumulated a lot of non-virtue or who have incomplete mental and physical faculties that make it difficult to practice the Dharma—it is said that the wearing of this mandala creates the condition for them to attain the three *kayas* in future lifetimes. If it is able to benefit such beings, then we should feel confident that it can help us as well.

The great master Longchenpa quoted the *Ratnakuta Sutra,* or the *Sutra of the Heap of Jewels,* which says that there are inconceivable benefits resulting from the use of mantras, different kinds of medicines, and other secret treatments. The mandala would certainly fall under the category of secret treatments. The buddhas' and bodhisattvas' methods to help beings, their meditative concentration and miraculous powers are inconceivable, so truly we cannot refute the idea that something could have this potential to benefit us.

Nonetheless, the benefits of wearing such a mandala depend a great deal on each person's faith and pure perception. Based on faith, things can benefit us that do not benefit people without faith. Accordingly, we must work on improving our faith each day until we have unshakeable confidence in the Three Jewels and in the path.

If a being is wearing the mandala at the time of death, the texts say that karma will be exhausted and the being will not have to circle in samsara for long. If the person who is dying does not have the empowerment and is not already wearing the mandala, you can place it on his or her body as soon as the senses begin to dissolve. You can even place the mandala on the heart of a pet who is dying; the power of dependent arising—when causes and conditions come together—is so truly amazing that even such a thing as liberation for a dog is possible.

Ideally, the mandala should remain directly on top of the heart for three days after the outer breath ceases and while the body is not moved. This allows the blessing to fully enter the person's body for purification. Although this may not be possible, we can do our best. This instruction should be given in our Dharma Wills, along with instructions for burning or burying the mandala with the body.

PART THREE

---∿---

Medical Considerations for the Buddhist Practitioner

14

BUDDHISM AND WESTERN SCIENCE

—⟋⟍—

MODERN SCIENCE OFFERS so many possibilities for treatment that have never been available before. For a Buddhist practitioner, the impact of these treatment options on our end-of-life practice requires serious consideration. To give these things due consideration, once again, we must honestly reflect on our own capacity for mind stability and shamatha meditation. Is our mind really stable during practice, or is it distracted? Our assessment of this will determine how to approach our death from a medical point of view.

Pain Medication at the Time of Death

Whenever I give teachings on preparing for death, I am frequently asked questions about the use of pain medication, life support, and organ donations, so I would like to address these here.

If we are in a great deal of pain and cannot reduce its intensity, then we will not be able to have any mindfulness. Although it is difficult to give general advice, I feel it is okay for us to take pain medication until there are signs of the dissolution of the elements. When you think, "I am going to die soon, definitely within several days or several hours," then I think you can consider stopping your medication.

Whether we can stop medication depends on our abilities as practitioners. If we have stable meditation, stopping pain medication is not a big problem; if we do not, a painkiller might actually provide more mind stability. If we stop taking medication but our mind is not stable, we could harm ourselves during the dying process by making ourselves incapable of having any mindfulness or aspirations for our future rebirth. So it is most important to evaluate our practice honestly and without any delusions.

When my root lama was in the hospital dying, he called the doctors and told them to take his IVs out. They didn't want to do it, but he said, "Take them out now, I am going to die." Then he sat in meditation, taught his final teaching for this life, and passed away. Nothing affects this kind of practitioner. His or her mind is very stable without any medication, but ordinary practitioners don't have that kind of stability.

If we want to be able to die without painkillers, then we should practice every day, focusing on being mindful at all times. We should always remember our meditation and our daily practice.

Sometimes students want to know if a person who is not an advanced practitioner and is on strong pain medicine will be conscious enough to hear prayers read to them, to hear reminders to practice, and be able to take advantage of these supports. The answer is that it is a little hard for such people to take advantage of them; strong medicine affects people's minds. And so we should read the texts and prayers many times over to people in this state. It is almost the same as trying to help someone who has already died. The teachings intended to benefit those already dead instruct us to get close to their ear and say their lama's name, or to read teachings very clearly over and over again. We should do something similar in the case of a practitioner on significant pain medication.

Life-Support Issues

Many practitioners choose to have an advance directive stating their wishes to die without life-support technology. If they have not written this directive or spoken to their families about this, they can end up in the hospital with such machinery. When this should be removed is an individual decision. Some people have the mental clarity to decide for themselves. They may think, "Now, there is no point to having these machines and I will just focus on my Dharma practice."

If a person is incapacitated, however, the decision will fall to the person specified in the advance directive, the living will; this person will have to decide if their loved one has a chance to recover and will have to watch closely for the signs of death. The exact timing of the signs depends on the individual, and can sometimes take some time, depending on how attached the person is to staying alive. If you are with someone at this time, you can help them by saying, "Now you are in the dying process. Remember your Dharma, remember your practice." Remind them that they are not alone in facing death. But regardless of the timing of the signs of death, when they appear, death will be soon. This would be an appropriate time to take them off the machines.

Preparing for Organ Donation

Many students feel that organ donation is an act of compassion, but wonder how this will affect their deaths. If you are mentally prepared and without self-attachment, donating your organs is an extremely virtuous bodhisattva activity. If you are not prepared, however, it could pose some difficulties. This is a complex issue; it again depends on the individual and their level of bodhichitta. Each person must decide what is right for them.

Organ donation is a wonderful thing because we are quite literally and directly giving part of our own bodies to sustain the life of another. If we truly have a strong desire to donate our organs, we should train in that motivation on a daily basis so that it becomes a strongly habituated aspiration. That way, we can avoid any negative emotional responses that could affect our ability to practice through the dying process. Remember that we continue to hear and think while there is still inner breath. In the bardo state, a person's consciousness is much more acute—so the need to train in this aspiration is very real.

If you wish to donate organs, you must have no doubt that this is your desired course, and you need to be able to use your practice to cut through afflictive emotions. There are three practices I strongly recommend to support the generosity, merit, and virtue of donating organs so that it becomes a true bodhisattva activity:

▸ *The practice of phowa.* If we are able to transfer our consciousness at the time of death, then there would be no attachment to our bodies if the organs are removed. Of course, if a realized master does phowa for us, there would be no difficulty at all.

▸ *The practice of chod or kusali tsok.* Kusali tsok is a practice similar to chod in which we offer our body to benefit sentient beings, so at the time of death we will have no desire toward our body or attachment to the organs being removed. For this, we should work with an authentic teacher who has mastered chod.

▸ *Daily practice of tonglen.* Practicing tonglen each day enables us to keep bodhichitta in our hearts.

When we write our Dharma Will, we would want to include our wish to donate our organs, and may want to write a statement reminding us of this wish to benefit other beings that can be read to us as we are dying (see Appendix III).

Other Considerations

Every death is unique, but there are many shared experiences on both the spiritual and physical levels. Western scientific literature has identified a number of physical expressions of the dying process that are typically addressed from a medical perspective. Recently, recognition of the need for spiritual care has increased. As I talk with Western doctors, nurses, and hospice workers, I am also aware that some suggestions to help the dying may seem at odds with Buddhist instructions. I would like to add some suggestions from a Buddhist perspective about dealing with certain physical or psychological symptoms, and also clarify some issues where Buddhist perspectives may differ from Western medical perspectives.

Increased Sleeping. As our body begins to shut down, we may spend more and more time sleeping. Entrusted Dharma friends should continue to read our practices in a normal tone of voice, sitting as close to us as possible. We will still be able to hear them and receive benefit.

Disorientation, Confusion, Delirium. People may not see, hear, or understand what is going on around them as they come closer to death. For some people, the mind can become very confused and unable to attend to what is happening around them. If we are in a confused mental state, entrusted Dharma friends or helpers who come into the room may be able to help us by identifying themselves before they begin to speak or read, and reminding us why they are there.

Restlessness/Agitation. As the level of oxygen decreases in our brain, symptoms of restless and repetitive motions may appear. If we are able to hold a mala, it may be helpful for entrusted Dharma friends to place it in our hand as they repeat mantras or recite texts. I suggest a special mala be placed in our Dharma Box in case our daily mala is not with us. It would be beneficial to have this mala blessed by a lama before it is placed in the box. Using a mala in daily practice will create a good condition to remind us of our practice when a mala is placed in our hand as we are dying.

I have heard from hospice workers and medical professionals that tranquilizing medication is commonly used to help with this type of restlessness. This should be addressed in our Dharma Will, explaining that we do not want to be in great discomfort but we also do not want our minds dulled unnecessarily. If these symptoms are strong and are not relieved by mantras or by having our texts read to us, we should give instructions on whether we are willing to try such medications. This is similar to the discussion on pain medication. If we are so restless or agitated that we cannot take advantage of our meditation practice, we may want to request that a minimal dose be tried. Then if we are more relaxed and able to pay attention to our practices, either our entrusted Dharma friends or medical representative can let our health care workers know this.

It is important to find that fine line between being unable to focus due to symptoms versus being overmedicated. Our entrusted Dharma friends should report to healthcare providers on how they see medication affecting us, and feel comfortable asking for changes that would be in accordance with the wishes of our Dharma Will.

Atypical Behavior. Due to the oxygen levels decreasing or to other processes deteriorating, we are told that we may display behavior that is not typical for us. We may say or do things that are aggressive or negative. Should this happen, our entrusted Dharma friends could recite the Avalokiteshvara mantra, OM MA NI PAD ME HUNG HRI, for a period of time until they see us settle down again.

Body Position. We discussed using the "lion's pose"—lying on our right side with our head to the north. However, in order to prevent bed sores and the pain of staying in one position, I understand that it is customary for the body to be repositioned every few hours. But, as we said earlier, it is important to be free to focus on practice and not distracted by pain; if we are not advanced practitioners, we should not be upset at being moved. Our entrusted Dharma friends should do their best to have our heads to the north, and, once they know we are very close to death, they should place us on our right side if at all possible. If for some reason we cannot be placed in that position, our entrusted Dharma friends can simply say, "Visualize yourself in the lion's pose, just as Buddha Shakyamuni was when he passed into paranirvana." That will be sufficient.

Touching. Students tell me that recent literature suggests holding the dying person's hand to help comfort them and let them know they are not alone, or even lying next to them in the bed and holding them. I am sure this advice is motivated by deep compassion; at the same time it could create strong emotions in the dying person. If this is the case, entrusted Dharma friends can explain to family and friends how this might affect us by increasing our attachment to our loved ones and distracting us from practice. Non-Buddhist family and friends need to know that this is not because we don't love them or want to have contact (see the sample Dharma Will in Appendix III). They can be reminded to lightly touch the top of our head, which will be beneficial to us and comforting for them to do.

Permission to Let Go. I understand that another part of recent care for the dying is letting the dying person know that it is okay for him or her to "let go." I think this is a good idea. Again, the focus of family and entrusted Dharma friends should be on doing everything possible for us to concentrate on our practices for the time of death so that we are not held back by worries about our loved ones. If our death is not sudden and we have awareness early in the dying process, or it is something we have asked our entrusted Dharma friends to do, it may be beneficial to arrange a time for a "goodbye ceremony." Family and friends can gather to say their goodbyes to us, express their love and gratitude, and state their aspirations for our journey ahead. We can express our gratitude for their love and care at that time. This may be a good time to read the aspiration prayer we have composed in our Dharma Will. With this completed, everyone can turn their focus to the task at hand and read prayers or support the entrusted Dharma friends in their work.

Seeing Loved Ones Who Have Died Before Us. Many hospice workers and students who have been with their loved ones while they were dying have told me that the dying person "sees" and talks to spouses, parents, and other loved ones who have already died. This is not common in Tibet, although some advanced practitioners may be aware of their lama's presence before they die.

Buddhist texts say, "Based on confusion, the bardo appears." The best thing we can tell the dying person is that, no matter what appears, all is arising from the mind. Whatever appears, it is important that there be no attachment or aversion. I feel it is important to direct the dying person's awareness back to his or her practice at all times.

PART FOUR

Buddhist Practitioners as Caregivers

15

THE ENTRUSTED DHARMA FRIEND

———— —ᚱᚱ— ————

As I'VE EMPHASIZED throughout this book, the entrusted Dharma friends will be at the dying person's bedside with full attention on the practices for the time of death. They will have trained in phowa, learned to recognize the stages of dissolution, and understood their friend's aspirations for the time of death. It is up to the entrusted Dharma friends to be reliable guides in accordance with their friend's Dharma Will.

The relationship between entrusted Dharma friends is based on a profound commitment. We must fully trust each other to carry out this commitment with great mindfulness, compassion, and wisdom. If we consider making such a commitment, we should set aside time for contemplation and an honest assessment of our bodhichitta, our ability to carry through on promises, and our life circumstances. After exploring all aspects of this commitment, if we wish to enter into such a relationship, we will not only be helping others die with the best possible opportunities for liberation, but we will find numerous benefits for our own practice at the time of death.

If, however, we find that it is not possible for us to make such a commitment at this time, we can still participate in supporting our Dharma brothers and sisters through the dying process with prayers, practices, communicating with sangha members, and help-ing with the many arrangements for memorial services and crema-tion or burial. This will also be a great service to the dying person and his or her family.

I have given much thought to using the word "friend" in this con-text, as its use in Western society is different from that in Tibet. In the West, having a close relationship with another person often includes sharing our innermost secrets, even though we may not consider the effect on the other person. In Buddhism, intimacy is more about putting the other person ahead of ourselves. It means we practice bodhichitta, and for the sake of others and the sangha, we take care of any personality conflicts. We need to understand the difference between a close personal friend and someone we would consider a *Dharma friend*. Even among Dharma friends, there are different lev-els of closeness.

We can think of a Dharma friend from the outer, inner, and secret points of view. From the outer point of view, a Dharma friend would be anyone who relies upon the teachings of Buddha Shakyamuni. Thus, this group is numerous, and they would be considered distant friends. From the inner point of view, Dharma friends would be any group of practitioners who receive general Mahayana teachings com-monly from the same teacher. These students would be considered close friends.

In terms of the secret point of view, students of the same teacher who rely on what is called "one mandala"—the same lama, the same shrine, the same ritual items, etc.—to receive general Vajrayana teachings and empowerments would be considered very close Dharma friends. Lastly, the *unsurpassable most secret* Dharma friends would be those students who rely on one teacher and one mandala to receive empowerments, upadesha instructions, and instructions on Mahamudra or Dzogchen.

When we choose an entrusted Dharma friend to help us carry out our Dharma Will and Dharma Vision, we want to ask someone from among these groups. I will say more about this below.

When we choose someone to help us die, we must reflect seriously on his or her qualities. Think about the habitual patterns of that person. Do they complete their Dharma activities? Do they follow through on commitments? Do they have the interests of the larger sangha at heart? Are they willing to take an honest look at themselves and improve their conduct?

We should have a pure relationship with the people we wish to assist us. Can they help us with the view at the time of death? Can they point us in the right direction? If something happens between us, would this person be willing to work on restoring their *samaya* in order to promote harmonious relations and the health of the lama and the community? Would they be likely to do this in a timely manner? Scriptures tell us that when we break our bodhichitta toward another or we have some resentment toward them, we should regret and purify it before the night ends. If we cannot, then we should do our best to resolve things within three days, but certainly within a month.

Students sometimes want to know if it is a good idea to choose a close friend to be an entrusted Dharma friend; they wonder if their feelings for this person will cause distraction or attachment at the time of death. You can discuss this together and then make a plan ahead of time in order to avoid this problem. One way to ensure everything goes smoothly is simply to strengthen your practice by regularly contemplating impermanence and death, and working hard to master cutting through the afflictive emotions that arise. This would help us assist our friend or family member at their time of death and also when they are assisting us at ours. On the other hand, if our friend's death is too painful and distracts us from focusing on the practices (or if our death is too painful for our friend), there are many other things to do to be of help besides sitting right by the bedside. For example, we could prepare meals, do tonglen or yidam practice while outside the room, or help with contacting our friend's spiritual friend to get advice and guidance. We may choose to have this more flexible understanding with someone we are close to; we can agree to give each other permission to help in less direct ways if either begins to feel that the emotions are distracting.

If the entrusted Dharma friend is unexpectedly unable to be at a person's bedside, they should still do the practices the person has requested from wherever they are. But even if they can arrive within the three days after death, they should try to do that. If there is a strong relationship, it really does not matter where a person is, though it is good to make every effort to be there. If the entrusted Dharma friend has a strong connection with a yidam practice and feels they can help the person with this practice, they may do that as well.

The attributes listed above are what we are looking for in an ideal entrusted Dharma friend, but we must balance this with realism. The most important thing is the commitment to work out any difficulties; with this commitment we can count on the relationship working out for everyone's benefit. We cannot expect perfection or be overly critical, or we will not find anyone to be an entrusted Dharma friend!

Core Practice Groups

I encourage my students to form core groups of practitioners who will commit to mastering phowa for themselves and others and serve as guides for the journey into death and the after-death bardos. Some students wish to have only one or two entrusted Dharma friends, while others feel comfortable in a somewhat larger group. Some students ask individuals or form groups where there is a mutual relationship to be entrusted Dharma friends for each other; others may find it difficult to make a mutual commitment for various reasons. Each person will need to give serious thought not only to the commitment required to be an entrusted Dharma friend but to Dharma practice in general as well.

Small groups will likely have fewer relationship issues, but this puts more demands on just a few people. In that case, we would need to call on the larger sangha for some tasks. A group of four to seven people would help ensure that at least some members will be at the bedside of the dying person and allow the entrusted Dharma friends to take turns and have time to rest; it is hard work to be a focused guide over a prolonged period of time. Forming a core group is likely to be an organic process that will naturally evolve as the first two members come together and commit to fulfilling this role.

In Tibet, we typically have only our closest Dharma friend assist us before and after death with phowa, reading texts, and reminding us of oral instructions. My root lama asked only one person to be with him at the time of death. After death, then other lamas and monks were invited to come and pray. But in the West, we may not be living in the same town, city, or even state; having more than one person we can trust to help us makes sense. Also, because we are planning ahead, many circumstances may arise in the future that would make it difficult for that one person to get to our bedside. They could become ill and disabled, or die before us.

We naturally have different relationships with different individuals. As a group comes together, there must be a strong emphasis on harmony and putting the common purpose of the group ahead of personalities. We must be able to keep our samaya with every member of the group, and each member must be willing to work through any differences for the sake of the group as a whole. Without a commitment to do this, the entire group could be harmed.

As a group forms, members should discuss together how conflicts will be handled. The teachings generally instruct us to tell another person of our regret when we have committed a negative action toward them. But in a small group, speaking openly of resentments toward a member could risk harming the rest of the group. We may decide it is better to speak only with the person in question if we are sure that will not be hurtful, or to privately do purification practices and express regret in front of a photo of our yidam deity or lama. If we are constantly working on having perfectly pure bodhichitta, then opportunities to break our samaya will not arise, or if they do, they will be quickly purified. The entire group must be committed to practicing bodhichitta.

Entire sanghas may choose to come together to train in phowa and the signs of death, and to give overall support to the core groups formed by their members. The sangha as a whole might decide to be a kind of general Dharma friend and offer prayers and practices for the dying person from their individual homes or Dharma Center. The sangha members can do phowa, recite the King of Aspiration Prayers, the Aspiration for Noble Excellent Conduct, Avalokiteshvara practice, and so on. They can also offer to help out with any needs of the family.

For entire sanghas to come together for this purpose, there must be a strong emphasis on community and harmonious relations. Feelings of competition or jealousy will not serve the higher purpose of the group. Each member of the larger sangha must therefore work on cutting through any of these feelings if he or she is not chosen for another member's core group. As we said, the core groups must necessarily be small enough for people to know each other's Dharma

Wills and to keep pure samaya. We should all aspire to have the other person's liberation come before our own personal feelings.

All of this is excellent practice for a sangha to take up and work through.

In the chapters on creating our Dharma Vision and Dharma Will, we spoke about the need for yearly assessment of our progress. The ideal would be for the core group to come together each year to do this work, renew bodhisattva and refuge vows together, practice phowa, and communicate any changes in the members' requests for assistance. At the very least, this should be done individually and the results shared among the group members.

If we can do this, perhaps harmony can spread from us into our families and communities. We must try.

Written and Oral Instructions from Our Lama

If we have received secret teachings from our lama, then we must ensure that we do not break the samaya that forbids explaining the meaning of a secret teaching to someone who has not been instructed in the teaching. Traditionally in Tibet we do not make many notes; only scholars do this and they give these notes only to their most trusted Dharma friend. Earlier I recommended that people condense their notes of such teachings into something meaningful that can be read to them at the time of death. However, the only person who can read this to us is someone who has also received these teachings from our lama—a person in the "unsurpassable most secret Dharma friend" category. Therefore, if you have received Dzogchen or Mahamudra teachings, it will be important to ensure that there is one designated person from your sangha who can do this for you. Thus, if you are choosing to have only one or two people assist you at the time of death and you have secret teachings you wish to have read to you, you will need to take this into account.

A copy of the condensed oral instructions we have received should be kept in our Dharma Box in a sealed envelope, clearly labeled with something like, "Do not read; for entrusted Dharma friend [name] only. Please honor this request." A copy should also be given to that person in the binder of prayers and texts we will give him or her as soon as we have completed our Dharma Box. Then it will still be possible for that person to read them to us over the phone in case they cannot get to our bedside. It is okay for others to hear these teachings being read, as a distinction is made between reading and hearing. In Tibet thousands of monks may be gathered to chant and pray, but only the lama reads the oral instructions.

In preparation for death, we should go through all the notes we have taken when listening to secret teachings, as well as any pictures of lamas or deities (unless we wish to give them to sangha or family members), and wrap and label them, "Please burn when I die." Instructions should be given to both a family member and an entrusted Dharma friend on where they can be found, and the entrusted Dharma friend should be in charge of burning them. Any computer files with these notes should be labeled as well so they can be deleted.

In Tibet, we burn anything in the Tibetan language as we consider the language sacred and it would be disrespectful to throw it away. After we burn sacred items, we generally put the ashes in water, but here in the West I think it is good to throw the ashes to the wind—in some kind of environmentally sensible way—and let the wind carry them away.

CONCLUSION

———〰———

MY GRANDMOTHER DIED a few years ago and I was sad. But I thought, "Everyone has to die. Now is not the time to be sad; now I am here for her and my family and it is the time to be supportive and practice for them." Also, my uncle was murdered some years ago. I had to go in and see him lying there with blood covering the floor. I had both anger and sadness. However, I immediately controlled my emotions and sat down to practice. I thought, " If I am sad and angry, what will happen to him? I must practice for him."

Sometimes students dismiss the first noble truth taught by Buddha Shakyamuni, the truth of the suffering of samsara. They think they have accepted it, but they don't really take the time to contemplate it fully. Most of us have a hard time believing that the nature of the world is suffering; in fact, we are generally attached to the opposite idea. We need to reflect upon the nature of samsaric suffering in a focused way.

Even King Trisong Detsen, who played a pivotal role in establishing Buddhism in Tibet, experienced strong emotions when his daughter died. He asked Padmasambhava to bring her back to life. Padmasambhava did indeed bring her back to life in order to give her the *Khandro Nyingthig* teachings. Soon after that, she died; karma cannot be changed. In this way, Padmasambhava gave us all great teachings on impermanence.

When we take the time to contemplate impermanence and the nature of suffering, it helps us as well as the person who is dying. When we are grieving, we should not push the feelings away, nor should we hold on to them. For the serious Buddhist practitioner, training in transforming afflictive emotions into wisdom is essential.

We may feel that we are suffering alone and that no one else knows how we are feeling. We may even resent seeing others who have not lost someone like we have, but we should remember that they may feel happy now, but they will certainly feel suffering at some point. Again, that is the nature of samsara; it is a common human experience.

Each time we meet someone, we should use the opportunity as an engaged meditation and generate compassion, knowing that everyone is going to experience the same suffering and loss at some point. This is the most powerful way to deal with grief.

All practitioners should think about being with someone at the time of death as a true bodhisattva activity. Whether or not that person is a Buddhist or someone we know, we can be with them as they die. Perhaps they are all alone. We do not need to talk to them about Buddhism or our practices. As long as they accept our being with them, we can practice and be of benefit.

Let me conclude with an aspirational prayer:

> *With bodhichitta in our hearts and the aspiration to walk the bodhisattva path, may we offer our services to those dying in whatever capacity we are able. May we approach our deaths with great confidence and help others to do the same. And,*

as we practice with great diligence and prepare ourselves for death, may our certainty in the view increase and may all benefit from our efforts.

ACKNOWLEDGMENTS

Thank you to my translator, Allison Graboski, and my student, Eileen Cahoon, without whom this book would not have been possible. Also, we thank all those students who offered their time and assistance, including Bea Ferrigno for her keen eye in editing despite injuries; Dori and Merit Bennet for assistance with legal issues; Ananda Badet for providing information about hospice; Joan Stigliani for editing advice; and Julie Benson for another keen eye in the final reading. Finally, thank you to Laura Cunningham and Josh Bartok and everyone at Wisdom Publications for your help in bringing this work to fruition.

May all beings benefit.

AFTERWORD

by Tulku Thondup

EVERY INDIVIDUAL is a composite of body and mind. The body is like a hotel where the mind—the consciousness—resides and functions as long as conditions allow. When the last moments of life arrive, the mind departs from the body and starts transmigrating from rebirth to rebirth, just as travelers move from one hotel to another. The body, however, dissolves into the earth and disappears forever.

Our identity—who we are—is our mind, not the belongings that we have collected every minute of our waking life, the loved ones in whom we have invested our energy, or even the body that we have cherished. The mind leaves behind all of that at the time of death. But our karma—the healthy and unhealthy deeds and their associated mental habits that we have stored as seeds in our mind-stream during our lifetime—will produce as its fruition a pleasant or unpleasant world around us and joyful or painful experiences in us.

The effects of loving thoughts, pure perceptions, and devotional energies today will produce pure lands and peace and joy tomorrow. Therefore, heartfelt meditations and prayers, even if they are simple in form, will change the qualities and habits of our minds now and will produce ultimate peace and joy in the future.

So imagine the image and presence of Amitabha Buddha, the Buddha of Infinite Light; imagine the light of all-knowing wisdom and unconditional love. Open your heart to him with devotion, joy, and trust and pray for his blessings for all. Receive the blessings in the form of wisdom light of unconditional love and share them with all. Purify and transform the whole universe into a world of blessing light of unconditional love, omniscient wisdom, and ultimate peace. When our minds are fully open to and deeply enjoying the qualities of the Buddha, the Buddha presence has awakened in our own hearts. Then, the whole universe will appear to us as the pure land. That is where we will take rebirth and from where we will serve many.

We pay great attention to the details of our daily life, but spare no thought for the life that comes after death, though it will be our never-ending future. Abu Patrul Rinpoche lamented,

> Whoever I look at, they are all about to die.
> Whoever I think about, they are all counting on living forever.
> Having seen such heart-rending phenomena,
> My mind has rushed to the mountain solitude [to meditate].

Tulku Thondup Rinpoche
The Buddhayana Foundation, USA.

APPENDIX I

BUDDHIST PRAYERS FOR THE TIME OF DEATH

THERE ARE MANY beautiful Buddhist prayers that can be recited for a person who is dying. They are too numerous to be included in this small volume and can be obtained from many sources. Examples of traditional prayers for the time of death are listed below. Bound volumes of practices and prayers are available from the Phowa Foundation (www.phowafoundation.org).

- ▶ Meditation on the Great Compassionate One (Avalokiteshvara)
- ▶ Phowa: Buddhahood without Meditation
- ▶ Bardo Prayers
- ▶ Vajrasattva Sadhana and 100-Syllable Mantra
- ▶ The Prayer of Kuntuzangpo
- ▶ The Amitabha Aspiration Prayer to be Reborn in Dewachen
- ▶ The Prayer of Excellent Conduct
- ▶ The Entrance to the City of Omniscience
- ▶ Prayer of Regret
- ▶ Dedication Prayers

Mantras and Names of the Buddhas to Recite to the Dying

▸ Avalokiteshvara (Tib. Chenrezig):
OM MA NI PAD ME HUNG HRI

▸ Vajrasattva (short version):
OM BENZA SATTO HUNG

▸ Amitabha Buddha:
OM A MI TA BHA HRI

▸ 100 Peaceful and Wrathful Deities:
OM AH HUNG/ BODHI TSITTA MAHA SUKA JANA DHATU AH/
OM RU LU RU LU HUNG JO HUNG

▸ Medicine Buddha (Sangye Menla):
TADYATA OM BHEKADZAYA BHEKADZAYA MAHA
BHEKADZAYA BHEKADZAYA RANDZA SAMUDGATE SOHA

Any other mantras the dying person has recited in his or her lifetime are also appropriate.

Appendix II

Documents to Prepare for Your Death

———※———

There are three documents we should prepare now for the time of death.

(1) A legal will with our wishes for property disbursement and similar legal matters. Each state gives information on the requirements for wills and sample forms. In some states a handwritten document is acceptable. It is important to know the laws and regulations for your state.

(2) A Dharma Will. Each state has different legal requirements, so it is important to make our Dharma Will comply with these requirements. For instance, we should know if our Dharma Will needs to be witnessed when we sign it or needs to be notarized. We must be sure that what we are requesting from our entrusted Dharma friends, especially about after-death care, can actually be carried out.

(3) A healthcare directive that can be executed independently of a legal will. This allows us to designate a power-of-attorney for health care or to name individuals to make healthcare decisions for us when we are incapable of doing so (copies should, of course, be given to these designated decision-makers and kept with our legal will). Our

healthcare directive should also include our wishes about organ donation.

Sample healthcare directive forms conforming to each state's statute can often be downloaded from that state's website, although most states will accept alternative forms.

If we already have a legally executed will, additions can only be accomplished by executing an amendment, or codicil. The legal will is something typically not read until after the time of death, so any additions (e.g. instructions for burial or cremation, which must be in our legal will to be in accordance with state law) regarding our care should be made known to our family and entrusted Dharma friends. They should have a copy of our Dharma Will, and other copies should be placed in our Dharma Box and attached to our legal will.

Appendix III

Sample End-of-Life Medical Instructions and Dharma Will

—⚏—

THE FOLLOWING is a sample of a healthcare directive concerning end-of-life care and medications, followed by a sample Dharma Will with addendums for entrusted Dharma friends, non-Buddhist friends and family members, instructions for cremation or burial, and charitable contributions. The writing of the healthcare directive is important for Buddhist practitioners, as our medical representative will need to understand our wishes very clearly for treatment options and medication. We need to plan ahead how to best use our practice when we are likely to be experiencing pain and discomfort.

One option is to designate an entrusted Dharma friend as a medical representative; he or she may have a better idea of what medical care will enable us to practice and take advantage of hearing our practices read to us. If we wish to do this, we will need to write this in the healthcare directive and discuss this with our families to help them understand our reasons. Family members could feel hurt by anyone outside the family taking on such a role in our death. We should clearly communicate that we will need someone to assess our pain in relation to our ability to practice, and that family members could be very emotional seeing us in pain and therefore unable to make such a decision. With clear communication, we can help those close to us understand that there are many other roles they can play to help us. This could actually relieve them of a very difficult decision.

Everyone should feel free to modify and add to these sample documents in whatever way they choose, as long as the Dharma Will is in accord with any state laws and regulations.

SAMPLE MEDICAL INSTRUCTIONS

These are the instructions to my designated medical representative(s) for my end-of-life medical care:

(1) I would like to use pain medication if I show signs of being in significant pain. Once it is clear that I have only a few days to live, I would like to be taken off the pain medication. If it becomes evident that I am then in too much pain to focus on my Dharma practice, please put me back on the least amount of medication that will alleviate the pain but allow me to be aware of the prayers and texts beings read at my bedside. I understand this will not be easy to determine, so I appreciate your doing your best.

(2) I do not wish to have treatment to prolong my life, such as feeding tubes, cardiopulmonary resuscitation, or ventilators unless it is clear there is hope of recovery with a decent quality of life to follow (i.e. my mental capacities intact).

(3) I wish to die at home if at all possible. Please make every effort to arrange this, but I understand if it is not possible.

(4) Other directives: *(include any arrangements for organ donation, any instructions concerning embalming, etc.)*

Sample Dharma Will

—⚮—

Full Legal Name
Address
Date of Birth

I. Designated Entrusted Dharma Friends

(1) The following entrusted Dharma friends have agreed to be with me during the dying process if at all possible. If I am unable to do so, they should be contacted immediately upon reading this.

Entrusted Dharma Friend name

_____

Address

_____

_____

_____

Contact information (phone, cell, pager, email)

_____

_____

_____

(Continue list of names)

II. At the Time of Death

(1) My designated entrusted Dharma friends should be allowed to be with me at all times during my dying process. They will be praying and performing Buddhist practices. They have been asked to set up

an altar for me in my room. They will assist my non-Buddhist friends and family members to understand what they can do to best help me during this time. I know this may be difficult for my health care workers, but I ask that they allow this support in the best way possible. I also ask that the altar set up by my entrusted Dharma friends be respected and left as they set it up and in a place where I am able to see it from my bed. When they are not with me, they may leave a CD of spiritual practices playing. I wish to have this on at all times. Please do not turn it off and please *do not* have a TV playing in my room, as this will distract me from focusing on my prayers.

III. Spiritual Counsel

I have asked my entrusted Dharma friends to contact a Buddhist lama at the appropriate time. He or she is permitted to be with me at any time.

IV. Care of my Body after Death

(1) It is very important to me on religious grounds that my body remain for three days, or as long as possible, without being moved. If this is impossible, I request that my family and entrusted Dharma friends have as much time as they can to complete certain prayers before my body is moved.

(If you have contacted a group such as Crossings or Natural Transitions [see Appendix IV] that will transport your body to your home for the three days, include all arrangements and contact information here.)

_____

_____

_____

(2) I wish to be cremated/buried (*cross out one*). I request that this not take place until the fourth day after my death if at all possible. If I have chosen cremation, my ashes should be given to:

Name _____

Relationship _____

Contact info _____

(3) I have spoken with the following crematorium or funeral home about my requests and they have agreed with them. I have attached Addendum III with the special requests for the crematorium or funeral home.

Please contact:

Name _____

Address _____

Contact info and person spoken with _____

I have asked my designated entrusted Dharma friends to help with these arrangements.

V. Charitable Contributions

(1) I have appointed a Power-of-Attorney in my Last Will and Testament and given instructions for the distribution of my wealth. I have also arranged for prayers and practices to be done on my behalf and on behalf of all those now in the bardo states. I have requested my entrusted Dharma friends to help carry out these arrangements by informing the lama or monastery of my condition throughout the dying process. The contact information for these prayers is included in Addendum I.

If I have not arranged this before my death, I designate the following person to make charitable contributions for prayers and practices to be recited for my benefit:

Name _____

Address _____

Contact information
(phone, cell, pager, email)_____

_____

I have designated in my will that a specific gift for the amount of $ _____ be given to _____.

I have notified my Power of Attorney to release these funds for this purpose. (*Prearranging this is the easiest way to ensure your wishes can be carried out. If not, designating the name and amount as a specific gift will allow for easier disbursal of funds.*)

Addendum IV to this Dharma Will is attached with my specific charitable requests.

Signature _____

Date _____

Witness_____

Date _____

Addendum I
Requests to my Entrusted Dharma Friends

I am grateful you have agreed to help me with one of the most important moments of my life. I hope you will be able to be at my bedside, but please know that if it is not possible, I will appreciate your prayers and practices from afar.

I. My Dharma Box
I have created a Dharma Box with everything you will need to assist me. The Dharma Box will be (give location) _____.
It will have a binder for you with my prayers and practices, items to set up an altar by my bedside, and the means to play a recording of phowa, mantras, and prayers by my lama. Whenever you are not able to be at my bedside, please play the recording so that I can hear it. If you feel it is appropriate and possible for me to use earphones when you are not there, a pair can be found in the Dharma Box.

I have requested (name)_____ to read my oral instructions as he/she was with me when receiving them. As instructed, he/she is the only one who can do this, although you may be there when they are read. Please do not discuss these teachings with anyone else, as it can be harmful to both of you.
*(Give instructions ahead of time to this entrusted Dharma friend
to burn all notes of secret teachings and where to find them, as well
as any computer files of notes that should be deleted.)*

II. My Dharma Vision
I am including here what I wrote about my "ideal" death from my Dharma Vision, so that you will have a clear idea of how I would like to die:

_____

III. Lama Contact

Please contact my lama as soon as possible to describe my condition and ask for his or her help.

(List all contact information and agreements you have already made together. Also list other lamas or spiritual teachers you wish to be notified either before or at the time of death.)

_____

_____

_____

If my lama is able to come to my bedside, I request that transportation and accommodations be provided for him/her using funds from my accounts. My Power of Attorney will be able to provide this. *(Be sure that you have written this in your legal will and discussed this with the designated person who has Power of Attorney. You may also decide to arrange this ahead of time with your lama.)*

IV. The Liberation-by-Wearing Mandala

You will find a mandala in my Dharma Box *(unless you have been given an empowerment and are already wearing it. If so, let your entrusted Dharma friends know what to do. These instructions will be given to you by your lama if you receive the empowerment).* This mandala is not to be shown to others, so please place it around my neck (wrapped as an amulet) as soon as the senses are dissolving and leave it there until my death and until my body is brought home or to a funeral home. After my body has been bathed and dressed and will no longer be disturbed, it should be unwrapped and placed over my heart area under my clothing. Please ensure it remains with me until I am cremated or buried, at which time it should be burned or buried with me, still positioned over my heart area.

V. Dutsi

While I am in the process of dying, I would like to have the blessing of the dutsi pills I have placed in my Dharma Box. Please put one in some water and let me drink it if I am able or otherwise just sip on it.

VI. Organ Donation

(If you have chosen to be an organ donor [see chapter 14] you may include a statement like the one below to be read to you.)

(1) I have asked that my healthy organs be donated at the time of my death. Please read the following statement to me before my outer breath ceases and again before the organs are removed:

"I can no longer sustain life and am ready to die. I have requested that my organs be donated. I do this for the benefit of all sentient beings and so that someone who needs life can continue to benefit others."

VII. After Death

(1) I have requested that my body be cremated/buried. If my lama can attend, he or she will conduct whatever ceremonies are appropriate. Please help him/her in whatever way is needed. If my lama cannot attend, please be sure he/she knows the time of burial/ cremation. If others are allowed to be at the cremation to pray, I would appreciate them doing so.

(2) A folder of prayers that may be recited at my cremation, burial, and funeral can be found in my Dharma Box. Any other prayers people wish to recite are most welcome; please encourage this so that everyone is comfortable.

(3) It is important that those attending any service for me understand how strong emotions can affect me in the bardos. You will find

a handout in my Dharma Box that can be given to people, or you may choose to read it at the beginning of the funeral service. (*You may use the beginning paragraphs of Addendum II to create this handout or write something yourself.*)

(4) I would like the food served at any gathering after my death to be vegetarian so that we all may benefit from observing the vow of non-harm.

(5) I have requested / would like to request that a gravestone with special Buddhist symbols be made for my gravesite. (*If you have instructions for a gravestone, list all information here.*)

(6) If, after the forty-nine days following my death, my family does not want to keep my Dharma items, please keep what you would like and distribute the rest to other practitioners.

Again, I give you my deep gratitude. Your compassion and commitment creates an opportunity to inspire an endless circle of generosity and bodhichitta. May we continue to serve together until samsara is empty!
(*Add anything else you would like to say to your entrusted Dharma friends in gratitude for their service.*)

Name _____

Date _____

ADDENDUM II

Information to Be Provided to Non-Buddhist Family and Friends

Buddhists believe there is a journey after death through transitional states called *bardos*. According to the way a person has led his or her life and according to their state of mind at the very moment of death, the bardo journey can be one of liberation from suffering or one that leads to rebirth in samsara, the cycle of birth and death.

For this reason, Buddhists prepare for death in their daily meditations and practices. Remaining in deep meditation at the time of death offers the greatest opportunity for liberation, or at least a very positive rebirth conducive to continuing their spiritual progress.

Buddhist teachings on dying encourage a quiet and peaceful environment in which the dying person can pray, meditate, recite mantras, and recall the important instructions given to them by their teachers. Most Buddhist practitioners have not reached a high enough level of stability in their meditation to be undistracted by the suffering or strong emotions of their family and friends around them. The greatest help you can give your loved one is to put aside your feelings of sadness and grief and add your prayers to theirs. Family and friends are encouraged to focus on positive feelings and prayers that are meaningful to them, whether sitting with their loved one or wherever they may be during the dying process. Please continue this for forty-nine days after death; this is the length of time most people travel through the bardos until they take birth once again.

Buddhist texts describe the consciousness of someone who has died and who is in the bardo state as ten times more acute than while living. When you express intense emotions about them, positive or negative, they will be affected and may be distracted from their meditation. Please do your best to think of the person's journey in the bardo states and focus on your prayers and aspirations for them to become enlightened. They have chosen a spiritual path to help all beings become enlightened and can do this work most effectively once they have reached their own enlightenment. This is a time to feel joyful for their willingness to undertake this path and to take this opportunity to increase your own compassion and loving-kindness.

If you have time before your loved one is close to death, it is suggested that you share together what is in your hearts and be sure there is no unfinished business. It is a great gift to help the dying person leave this world with no regrets and for them to know that, despite your sadness, you will be okay. Then you can focus on the prayers that will benefit your loved one most at this time.

Your loved one has designated entrusted Dharma friends, Buddhist practitioners who have agreed to help them fulfill their spiritual wishes for the time of death. These people will be reading the practices and instructions that have been requested, and they may have been asked to contact your loved one's teacher(s). They will also be setting up an altar by the bedside as requested.

Prayers from all traditions will be beneficial. Please do what is comfortable for you. If you would like to use prayers from the Buddhist tradition, the entrusted Dharma friends will have copies of prayers chosen by your loved one.

Addendum III
Instructions for Burial or Cremation

(1) If my body must be moved after death, my preference is for it to be at home for three days. I prefer not to be embalmed but that my body be kept on ice or dry ice for the three days. Please keep my body clean during this time.

(2) The following is a list of the prayers I wish to have recited at my burial or cremation. Copies can be found in my Dharma Box and

can be distributed to those attending. Any other prayers my family or friends wish to recite are welcome. I would like the CD of mantras used while I was dying played in the background of any funeral service.

(List the prayers you wish to be recited and which CD to be used.)

(3) I would like the following ritual objects to be buried or cremated with me:

(List the items and where they will be found.)

(4) Include any other instructions for this time.

ADDENDUM IV
Charitable Contributions

(Your legal will should contain instructions for the disbursal of your possessions, but it may not be read for some time after your death. Here you can reiterate your contributions for spiritual purposes to ensure a timely donation if you are requesting a lama or monastery to perform phowa on behalf of yourself and all beings in the bardo. It is strongly recommended that you arrange for this ahead of time so that phowa is performed at the optimal time. Once you have made arrangements, include the contact information and when to call them. If you have not already made offerings for these services, include information on how funds are to be obtained from the person acting as Power of Attorney. Please seek legal help for any questions you have about your list of contributions.)

RESOURCES FOR LEGAL WILLS, HEALTHCARE DIRECTIVES, AND AFTER-DEATH CARE

—⁂—

THERE ARE MANY resources available today that offer instructions and advice on advance directives and wills, as well as sample legal forms. The following is necessarily limited information; it is important to support your choices with up-to-date research.

Here are a few:

The American Hospital Association: Put It in Writing—
www.putitinwriting.org
This site gives information on advance directives and state-by-state regulations. They have a wallet ID card for download, advising that you have made advance directives and who to notify in an emergency. They also answer many FAQs.

Aging with Dignity: Five Wishes—www.agingwithdignity.org
The *Five Wishes* document is currently valid in forty states and helps you create a will that includes medical directives and spiritual care.

National Hospice and Palliative Care Organization
www.caringinfo.org

The following websites offer information on home-based after-death care, planning home funerals, and arranging for transport of the body to and from hospital/home/crematorium:

Crossings: Caring for our Own at Death—www.crossings.net

Natural Transitions—www.naturaltransitions.org

Final Passages—www.finalpassages.org
(includes a link to a book available on the laws of all states)

Undertaken with Love—www.undertakenwithlove.org

ANYEN RINPOCHE'S
LONGCHEN NYINGTHIG LINEAGE

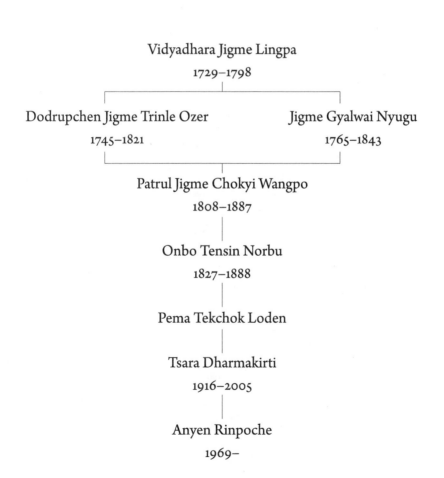

Vidyadhara Jigme Lingpa

1729–1798

Dodrupchen Jigme Trinle Ozer

1745–1821

Jigme Gyalwai Nyugu

1765–1843

Patrul Jigme Chokyi Wangpo

1808–1887

Onbo Tensin Norbu

1827–1888

Pema Tekchok Loden

Tsara Dharmakirti

1916–2005

Anyen Rinpoche

1969–

Appendix VI

The Meaning of Samaya

—∞—

In Vajrayana Buddhism, we talk about *samaya*—vows or commitments—that ensure we keep our conduct and practice pure. This is an immense topic as there are millions of samayas, but they can all be condensed into the *Five Root Samayas*, whose foundation is Shantideva's teachings in *The Way of the Bodhisattva*.

The first root samaya is to never lose our bodhichitta even for an instant. To miss this first samaya would be like an animal losing one of its legs or a car missing one of its wheels. Our practice cannot flourish without bodhichitta. The second vow is to regard our teacher as the Buddha, and for this we must strive to have pure perception. We should train in thinking that all beings have buddha-nature. Whenever we feel agitated with someone, we can focus on their buddha-nature, even if we are unable to see them as an actual buddha.

The third root samaya is to take up our yidam practice regularly, from six practice periods every day to at least one time a month. I recommend to my students that they do yidam practice daily. The fourth is to have harmonious relationships with and respect for all our Vajra brothers and sisters.

The fifth root samaya is to refrain from speaking the secret meaning of a teaching to someone who has not received the teaching, including our spouses. If a lama gives us a secret teaching and asks us not to share it, then we must not. The lama may give us permission to do so if he or she has a relationship with someone we are close to; otherwise we will be breaking our root samaya. If we speak about the teaching, it will affect not only everyone who received that teaching but the teacher as well.

We should reflect on these five root samayas and consider how effective we have been at keeping them. If we feel we have had some fault, then it is important to change our conduct. Keeping our samaya purely will act as a natural support for our meditation and the meaning of the teachings will become apparent to us. Those who do not keep their samaya may have some initial experiences of the view, but over time their meditation does not seem to improve.

Even in our worldly lives, we make many promises we know we cannot keep. We must think more carefully before doing this. A bodhisattva does not make many promises, but after considering the implications of a promise and accepting that promise, he or she will be sure to fulfill it. There is a metaphor given in the teachings for the bodhisattva's commitment—it is as if the promise is written in stone; even death cannot stand in the way of completing that action. So we must reflect deeply on our commitments.

When we make a mistake or break a promise, we should make every effort to repair it. The logic behind taking the bodhisattva vow is to have an overlying and long-term commitment to completing the bodhisattva path. We know that if we make a mistake, we can turn to the teachings to show us how to restore our vow.

INDEX

—◦◦◦—

A

Abu Patrul Rinpoche, 136
accidents, 82
advance directives (living wills), 115
after-death care, resources for, 155–56
agitation, 79, 118
AH syllable, xi
Akshobhya, 69
all-pervasive energy, 53
Amdo province, 162
American Hospital Association, 155
Amitabha, 69, 87–89, 104–5, 136–37
  aspiration prayer, 137
  mantra, 138
Amitayus, 89–90
Amoghasiddhi, 69
anger, 29, 60, 63
  phowa practice and, 80
  at the time of death, 95
animal realms, 69
animals, beloved, death of, 30, 109
appearance stage, 60–61, 67–68, 80

aspiration prayers, 26, 105, 120, 128, 131–32. *See also* prayers
attachment, 28, 69, 70
  phowa practice and, 85, 80, 94
  at the time of death, 96
  visions of white light and, 60–61
attainment stage, 61–64, 67–68, 80
atypical behavior, 118–19
Avalokiteshvara, 84, 104, 105
  mantra, 119, 138
  practice, 128
aversion, 69, 70, 71

B

bardo states, xv, 2, 36
  Bardo of Birth and Living, 43–46, 66
  Bardo of Dying, 46–47, 53, 58–59, 68, 72, 76
  Bardo of Existence, 73–74, 78
  Bardo of Meditative Concentration, 44, 45–46
  Bardo of Suchness, 65–69, 72–73

core practice groups and, 126–27
five days of meditative concentration and, 69–71
liberation in, after death, 65–74
overview, 43–47, 151
stages of dissolution and, 49–50
the three days following death
and, 105
Beacon of Certainty (Miphan
Rinpoche), 63
birth. See also karma; rebirth
contemplation of, 31
Bardo of Existence and, 73
phowa practice and, 77–78, 79
blinding lights, experience of, 70, 71
blood flow, 54–58, 62
bodhichitta, 67, 70, 103, 106, 128, 132
described, 24–25
Dharma friends and, 123–25
Dharma Visions and, 24–25
dissolution of elements and,
56–57
organ donation and, 115
phowa practice and, 81, 82, 84,
89–90, 93
power of, 67
sayamas and, 159
tonglen and, 97
vows, 99
bodhisattva(s), 132, 159–60
mandalas and, 109
phowa practice and, 77–80, 87,
93–94
tulkus and, 74
vows, 93, 129
body. See also breath; channels;
sense experience

blood flow in the, 54–58, 62
care of, after death, 33–35, 144–45,
148–50, 152–53
dissolution of elements and,
52–59
during death, 95, 119
essence, 72
filling with light, 60
phowa practice and, 78–91, 95
rainbow, 13, 16–17
Bon masters, 16
breath
cessation of, 59–60
dissolution of, into consciousness, 57–58
inner, 2, 58–60, 81, 82
outer, 58, 59, 70, 76, 80, 81, 99
Buddha
death of, 95, 119
Dharma friends and, 124
first noble truth taught by, 131
names of, to recite to the dying,
138
buddha-nature, 63, 68–69, 76, 159
Buddhayana Foundation, 136
burial, 35, 82, 145, 149–50, 152–53

C
channels, 54–58, 61–62
cessation of inner breath and,
59–60
phowa practice and, 78–81, 84,
86–91
charitable contributions, 34, 36,
145–46, 153
chi (energy), 54, 57
Chinese medicine, 54

chod practice, 58, 66, 82, 116
compassion, 102, 123, 132
  anger and, 29
  bardo states and, 66–67, 73, 74
  Dharma Visions and, 22, 25
  dreams and, 67
  for dying persons who are not
    Buddhist, 106
  phowa practice and, 77–78, 81,
    84, 87
concentration
  five days of meditative, 69–71
  phowa practice and, 81
confidence, 16–17, 22, 66–67, 75, 109
confusion, 117
consciousness, 14, 82. See also mind
  Bardo of Suchness and, 68–69
  dissolution of, 57–58, 62, 67
  transference of, 5
core practice groups, 126–29
cremation, 35, 104, 124, 145, 149–50
  instructions, 152–53
  signs at the time of, 13
  sudden death and, 82
Crossings: Caring for our Own
  Death Web site, 156
cutting through, practices of, 64

D
Dedication Prayers, 137
delirium, 117
desire, 63, 80
Dharma Box, 22–24, 94, 147
  Dharma Will in, 34
  dutsi in, 95, 149
  malas in, 118
  mandalas in, 148

oral instructions in, 130
overview, 6, 37–40, 139
prayers in, 26, 98, 149, 152–53
Dharma friends, 22–24, 34–35,
  123–30
  bardo states and, 70
  core practice groups and, 126–29
  phowa practice and, 75, 93, 90, 95
  role of, 6
  signs of death and, 51, 52, 55
  three-ring binders for, that hold
    practices, 38
  unsurpassable most secret, 124
Dharma Vision, 44, 49–64, 125, 147
  aspiration prayers as part of,
    97–98
  contemplation and, 24–26
  creating, 19–32
  described, 5–6
  ground luminosity and, 64
  need for, 20–22
  phowa practice and, 75
  revising, 32
Dharma Will(s), 22–24, 95, 125,
  139–40. See also wills
  annual review of, 38
  aspiration prayers and, 120
  instructions for the handling of
    the body after death in, 103, 116
  mandalas and, 110
  overview, 5–6, 33–36
  sample, 141–53
Dharmakaya, 5, 62, 67–68, 72,
  76–79, 86
disorientation, 117
dissolution, stages of, 49–54
Dorje Chodpa practice, 82

Dorlo Rinpoche, 65
downward-cleansing wind, 53
Dra Talgyur Root Tantra, 108
Dream Bardo, 44, 45, 66, 73–74. *See also* Dreams
dreams, 66–67, 72–74, 77. *See also* Dream Bardo
dutsi (blessed pills), 39–40, 95, 149
Dzogchen teachings, 1, 14, 15, 124, 129
    attachment and, 51
    bardo states and, 46, 66
    Dharma Vision and, 21, 26
    four types of liberation and, 72

E
earth element, 52–55
elements, dissolution of, 52–59
emptiness, 68, 72, 84
end-of-life medical instructions, 139–53
enlightenment. *See also* liberation
    Dharma Visions and, 20, 22, 24–25
    phowa practice and, 79
Entrance to the City of Omni-science, 137
environment, for death, preparing, 94–96
equality, state of, 79

F
fainting, 14
faith, 22, 74, 75, 87, 109
fasting, 105
fear, 66–67, 70, 71
    confidence without, attaining, 66–67

at the time of death, 95, 100
feminine energy, 61
Final Passages, 156
fire element, 55–57
five shandkas, 68–69
Five Wisdom Buddhas, 69–71
Five Wishes document, 155
form
    Bardo of Suchness and, 68–69
    generation stage yoga and, 72
Four Mind Turnings, 45–46
four noble truths, 131
full attainment stage, 67–68, 80
funeral services, 149–50. *See also* burial

G
generosity, 28–29, 36
goodbye ceremony, 120
gravestones, 150
grief, 30–31
ground luminosity, 62–64, 66, 68, 76. *See also* luminosity
guru yoga, 74

H
hands, holding, 119
head, focus on the top of, 28, 55, 99–100
healthcare directives, 139–53, 155–56
heart, 57, 58, 61, 62
    centers, 70, 87, 89, 108
    mantras, 74
    phowa practice and, 80
Heart Sutra, 82
hell realms, 69
HI-KA syllables, 88–89

home alters, 94
hospice workers, 102, 117, 118, 120
HRI syllable, 87, 99
HUNG syllable, 74
hungry ghosts, 69

I
increase, stage of, 61, 67–68
inner breath, 2, 58–60, 81, 82. *See also* breath
intermediate states, 2

K
karma, 68–69, 70, 74
  cho practitioners and, 58
  contemplation of, 31
  generosity and, 36
  mandalas and, 109
  Padmasambhava and, 131–32
  phowa practice and, 78, 98
  Thondup on, 135–36
kayas, 109
Khandro Nyingthig teachings, 131–32
King of Aspiration Prayers, 128
King Trisong Detsen, 131
Kuntuzangpo Prayer, 100, 103, 137
kusali tsok, 116
Kyabje Tsara Dharmakirti Rinpoche, 6, 75

L
Lama Chupur, 1–2
legal wills, 33, 115, 139–40, 155–56
let go, permission to, 119–20
Lhakto, Pasang, 1
liberation. *See also* enlightenment

bardo states and, 72, 74
four types of, 72
mandalas and, 107–10
phowa practice and, 77, 80
Liberation-by-Wearing Tantra, 107–10
life-support issues, 59, 115
light, visions of, 60–61
Lingpa, Tsasum, 55–58
lion's pose, 95, 119
living wills (advance directives), 115
Longchen Nyingthig lineage, 6, 75, 83, 88, 156
Longchenpa, 26, 46, 108, 109
lotus petals, 86
loved ones
  death of, contemplating, 30–31
  who have died before us, seeing, 120
loving-kindness, 22, 66, 106
luminosity
  of appearance, 60–61
  of attainment, 62
  Bardo of Suchness and, 67–69
  empty, 60
  ground, 62–64, 66, 68, 76
  of increase, 61
  phowa practice and, 87

M
Madhyamika, 63
Mahamudra, 14, 124, 129
Maitreya, 79
malas, 39, 118
mandalas, 40, 95, 107–10, 124
mantras, 40, 74, 118–19, 138
  Avalokiteshvara, 119, 138

at funeral services, 153
generation stage yoga and, 72
mandalas and, 109
OM (long-life), 90
phowa practice and, 90
during the three days following
  death, 103, 104
masculine energy, 60
Medicine Buddha, 100, 105, 138
meditation, 24–25, 60, 132
  bardo states and, 66, 69–71
  Dharma Visions and, 20–21
  phowa practice and, 77–78
  rooms, thangkas in, 74
*Meditation on the Great Compas-
  sionate One*, 84, 137
metaphors, transference based on
  three, 78–80
Middle Way philosophy, 63
Milarepa, 26, 78
mind
  appearances arising from the, 100
  Bardo of Suchness and, 67–69
  mastering the, importance of, 30
  phowa practice and, 77, 79, 81,
    83–85, 96–98
  preparing, for the time of death,
    96–98
  stabilizing the, 66–67
mindfulness, 11–17, 64, 73, 74, 123
  luminosity of attainment and, 62
  pain medication and, 113
  signs of dying and, 54–55
Mipham Rinpoche, 63
moon, symbolism of, 60

N
Nagarjuna, 63
National Hospice and Palliative
  Care Organization, 155–56
National Transitions, 156
near-death experiences, 2–3
ngondro, 45–46
Nirmanakaya phowa, 72, 77–78. *See
  also* phowa practice

O
OM (long-life) mantra, 90. *See also*
  mantras
100 Peaceful and Wrathful Deities
  prayer, 138
organ donation, 115–17, 149
Orgyen Khamdroling, xv, 162
outer breath, 58, 59, 70, 76, 80, 81,
  99. *See also* breath

P
Padmasambhava, 65, 81–82, 85,
  131–32
Padmatso, Kaki, 1
pain medication, 113–14, 118
parents, choosing, 73–74
Patrul Rinpoche, 87
*Peaceful and Wrathful Liberation
  Upon Hearing* (Lingpa), 55
PHET syllable, 91
*Phowa Buddhahood without Medita-
  tion*, 83–91, 137
Phowa Foundation, xv, 7, 40, 82,
  137, 161–62
phowa practice, 5, 7, 40, 45, 103
  when death is near, 93–100
  Dharma Wills and, 34

Nirmanakaya, 72, 77–78
for others, 80–82
groups, xiv
instructions, 83–91
organ donation and, 116
overview, 75–82
preparation for, 83–85
Power of Attorney, 139–40, 146, 148, 153
prayer(s)
aspiration, 26, 105, 120, 128, 131–32
dedication, 137
in Dharma Boxes, 26, 98, 149, 152–53
of Excellent Conduct, 137
Kuntuzangpo, 100, 103, 137
100 Peaceful and Wrathful Deities, 138
overview of, 137–38
of Regret, 137
predictions, of one's own death, 13
pujas, 104
pure land, 79
pure realm, 85–91
purification rituals, 34

R
rainbow body, 13, 16–17
rangdrol, 64
rangsel (luminous beads), 13
Ratnaketu, 100, 109
Ratnakutu Sutra (Sutra of the Heap of Jewels), 109
Ratnasambhava, 69
rebirth, 3, 73, 77–78, 114. See also birth; karma
refuge, taking, 99

restlessness, 118
rigpa, 16
Rupakaya, 72

S
sadhanas, 84
Samantabhadra, 68, 95, 108
Samantabhadhri, 68, 108
samayas, 44, 125, 129, 159–60
Sambhogakaya, 67, 72, 77, 89, 108
samsara, 12, 72, 109, 132, 150
sangha, 23, 94, 124, 129
Secret Mantrayana teachings, 44, 77, 108
seed syllable AH, xi
sense experience, 50–52, 62, 68–69
shamatha, 63
Shantideva, 159
Six paramitas, 28–29
six realms, of sentient beings, 69
sleep, 66, 97–98, 117. See also dreams
spleen, 54, 55
stupas, 16, 108
sudden death, 82
suicide, 82

T
tai chi, 83
Tara, xi
thangkas, 70, 74, 87, 94, 95
Thondup, Tulka, 135–36
Three Jewels, 22, 109
three kayas, xi, 109
three poisons, 80
Tibet, 66, 82, 94, 120, 124, 127
Tibetan Book of the Dead, The, 14, 43, 99

descriptions of the Bardo of
Suchness in, 65
use of, during the three days following death, 103, 105
tonglen, 26, 67, 96–98
Dharma friends and, 126
organ donation and, 115
for someone who is dying, 101–2
transference, based on three metaphors, 78–80
trust, 2, 21–22
Tsara Dharmakirti Rinpoche, ix–xi
tulkus, 74, 77–78

U
Undertaken with Love Web site,
156
upadesha instructions, 124
upward-moving wind, 53
Uttaratantra Sutra, 63

V
Vairochana, 69
Vajrakilaya, 67, 82
Vajrasattva, 74, 104–5, 137–38
Vajrayana, 77, 78, 124

Vajrayogini, 85–91
vegetarianism, 104–5, 150
Vidyadhara Lama, 55, 57, 58

W
water element, 54–56
Way of the Bodhisattva, The (Shantideva), 159
wills. See also Dharma Will(s)
advance directives, 115
legal, 33, 115, 139–40, 155–56
wind element, 53, 56–58, 60
wind energy, 53–55, 84, 87
Words of My Perfect Teacher (Patrul
Rinpoche), 87

Y
Yeshe Tsogyal, 85
yidam deities, 72, 74, 77, 94–95, 128
yidam practice, 77, 93–95, 105, 126,
159
yoga, 13, 26, 72, 108
guru, 74
phowa practice and, 83
uncommon (delogs), 65

About the Phowa Foundation

———— ∿ ————

THE PHOWA FOUNDATION supports the vision of Anyen Rinpoche to help sentient beings around the world in the dying process. Phowa is a traditional practice that is performed by all Tibetan Buddhist lineages and can benefit all beings, Buddhist or non-Buddhist. It helps the dying person create favorable conditions for liberation or a positive rebirth. Phowa can be done for animals as well, to help them connect with the Dharma in a future life.

One of the Foundation's primary goals is to establish an ongoing meditation retreat of monks and nuns in Tibet whose sole mission is the practice of phowa and purification practices for those who are dying or have died. Phowa and related practices may be requested for oneself or a loved one for up to forty-nine days. In the US, Anyen Rinpoche and qualified practitioners also practice phowa and other rituals for the dying.

The Phowa Foundation also offers education on death and dying, retreats for training in phowa and becoming an entrusted Dharma friend who helps others through the dying process, prayer books and items such as liberation-by-wearing mandalas, blessed pills, and gravestone designs. The Foundation website allows students to ask questions of Anyen Rinpoche about the dying process and to receive updated information on such services as after-death care and home funerals. A long-term goal of the organization is to establish extended phowa retreats for Western students and a hospice that will provide a supportive environment for Buddhist practitioners while dying.

The Phowa Foundation is a special project of Orgyen Khamdroling, a nonprofit organization that supports the culture and spiritual tradition of Tibet. Among other projects, Orgyen Khamdroling sponsors Tibetan children in rural parts of Amdo province to attend school, as well as a girls' literacy clinic. A future goal is the establishment of a boarding school where village children can be educated in their traditional culture as well as become bilingual in both Tibetan and Chinese.

For more information on services provided by the Phowa Foundation, please visit www.phowafoundation.org. Information on Orgyen Khamdroling's projects and events as well as Anyen Rinpoche's teaching schedule can be found at www.anyenrinpoche.com.

About the Author

---—〰—---

ANYEN RINPOCHE was born in Amdo, Tibet, and his Dharma lineage can be traced back directly to the renowned Dzogchen master Patrul Rinpoche. After more than fourteen years of extensive study and solitary retreat, he earned the degree of *khenpo* (master teacher) and became the head scholar of his monastic university. He has taught extensively in Tibet and China and now mentors students throughout Southeast Asia, Japan, and North America. He lives in Colorado.

About the Translator

ALLISON CHOYING ZANGMO is a student of Anyen Rinpoche and his root master, Tsara Dharmakirti Rinpoche. She has been studying Tibetan language and Buddhism under Anyen Rinpoche's personal guidance for the past ten years. She is Anyen Rinpoche's personal translator for both Dharma talks and textual translations. She lives in Denver, Colorado.

About the Editor

EILEEN CAHOON was a clinical psychologist for twenty years and worked with many terminally ill patients before devoting full-time attention to Dharma projects and study. Helping people through the dying process has been a long-term interest. Eileen began studying with Anyen Rinpoche shortly after his arrival in the U.S. She lives in Albuquerque, New Mexico.

Also by Anyen Rinpoche

—⟋⟍—

Living and Dying with Confidence
A Day-by-Day Guide
Anyen Rinpoche and Allison Choying Zangmo

"Anyen Rinpoche has skilfully woven the dharma teachings into these everyday contemplations on death which will be very beneficial especially for those in denial or dealing with loss."
—Tenzin Palmo, founder of Dongyu Gatsal Ling Nunnery

Journey to Certainty
The Quintessence of the Dzogchen View:
An Exploration of Mipham's Beacon of Certainty
Anyen Rinpoche and Allison Choying Zangmo

"Remarkably accessible, this book is essential reading for anyone attempting to understand or practice Dzogchen today."
—John Makransky, author of *Awakening Through Love*

Momentary Buddhahood
Mindfulness and the Vajrayana Path
Anyen Rinpoche
Foreword by Tulku Thondup Rinpoche

"An extraordinary book."
—Deborah Schoeberlein, author of *Mindful Teaching and Teaching Mindfulness*

Also available from
Wisdom Publications

—❧—

Lessons from the Dying
Rodney Smith
Foreword by Joseph Goldstein

"*Lessons from the Dying* could also be called 'lessons for the living' because of the courageous honesty revealed in so many of the stories told here... It is a wise and gentle reminder of the great mystery that illuminates life."
—Joseph Goldstein, author of *One Dharma* and *A Heart Full of Peace*

Buddhist Care for the Dying and Bereaved
Jonathan S. Watts
Yoshiharu Tomatsu

"A valuable and amazing resource! This collection is a 'must' for those of us involved in chaplaincy care."
—Pat Enkyo O'Hara, guiding teacher, New York Zen Center for Contemplative Care

Medicine and Compassion
A Tibetan Lama's Guidance for Caregivers
Chökyi Nyima Rinpoche with David R. Shlim, MD
Foreword by Harvey Fineberg and Donald Fineberg

"I was dumbfounded by how much Chökyi Nyima Rinpoche comprehends the emotional challenges facing doctors in relationship to their patients. He nails it time and time again. Magnificent! I shall continue to reread it just for the pleasure of the teachings, for the clarity of his mind, and the purity of his heart. This is a very worthy project."
—Jon Kabat-Zinn, MD, author of *Full Catastrophe Living* and *Wherever You Go, There You Are*

How to Be Sick
A Buddhist-Inspired Guide for the Chronically Ill and Their Caregivers
Toni Bernhard
Foreword by Sylvia Boorstein

"Full of hopefulness and promise… this book is a perfect blend of inspiration and encouragement. Toni's engaging teaching style shares traditional Buddhist wisdom in a format that is accessible to all readers."
—*The Huffington Post*

About Wisdom Publications

Wisdom Publications is the leading publisher of classic and contemporary Buddhist books and practical works on mindfulness. To learn more about us or to explore our other books, please visit our website at wisdompubs.org or contact us at the address below.

Wisdom Publications
199 Elm Street
Somerville, MA 02144 USA

We are a 501(c)(3) organization, and donations in support of our mission are tax deductible.

Wisdom Publications is affiliated with the Foundation for the Preservation of the Mahayana Tradition (FPMT).